Great Insults
and
Comebacks

Verbal Victory for All Occasions

NEW
HOLLAND

Frank Allen

First published in Australia in 2008 by
New Holland Publishers (Australia) Pty Ltd
Sydney • Auckland • London • Cape Town

1/66 Gibbes Street Chatswood NSW 2067 Australia
218 Lake Road Northcote Auckland New Zealand
86 Edgware Road London W2 2EA United Kingdom
80 McKenzie Street Cape Town 8001 South Africa

A record of this book is held at the National Library of Australia

ISBN: 9781741106459

Publisher: Fiona Schultz
Designer: Natasha Hayles
Managing Editor: Lliane Clarke
Production Assistant: Liz Malcolm
Printer: McPhersons Printing Group, Maryborough, Victoria

10 9 8 7 6 5 4 3 2 1

Contents

Introduction

The best insults leave us feeling, 'I wish I'd said that!' Anyone can use a four-letter word, but I hope that in the following pages you'll find some elegant examples of verbal nastiness to give you something to aspire to. There's a world of difference between a finely honed insult and the sort of second-rate cursing and abuse that you often hear.

Just for the record—an insult is a verbal attack. It's designed to be taken personally. A put down is a generally disparaging remark (often liberally laced with sarcasm and irony) and a calumny is an assault on someone's reputation. The important thing is that a good insult is one that makes you laugh, or at least raises a smile.

Louis Nizer was a UK-born, US lawyer who put his skill with words to good use in the courtroom. His A-list clients included Charlie Chaplin, Salvador Dali and Mae West. He once observed that: 'A graceful taunt is worth a thousand insults.'

Here, I hope that I've gathered some of the most graceful taunts and insults ever recorded. Paraphrase them and adapt them freely, but save them for only the worthiest adversary. And if you ever catch someone out using something on you that you've heard before, just use Irish novelist Jonathan Swift's classic rejoinder: 'Fine words! I wonder where you stole them.' Here is my favourite insult:

In 1763 the English radical politician and journalist John Wilkes published a poetic parody of Alexander Pope's *An Essay on Man* called *An Essay on Woman*. Wilkes' essay was considered pornographic and obscene and, among other things, it earned Wilkes the everlasting enmity of the Earl of Sandwich. One day the two men met accidentally.

SANDWICH: Sir, you will die either of the pox or on the gallows.

WILKES: That, my lord, depends on whether I embrace your lordship's mistress, or your principles.

I wish I'd said that.

1. The famous and their professions

The famous and would-be famous are fair game. Anyone who wants a public life or a public profession has got it coming to them and the famous not only have to take it, they're also not shy about dishing it out. Whether famous or aspiring to fame, it helps to have the hide of an elephant.

• • • • • • •

Actors, directors, filmmakers

Paradise with a lobotomy.
Anonymous, on Hollywood

She has all the emotion of a goal post.
Anonymous, on Linda Evans

Television: the bland leading the bland.
Anonymous

She reminds me of those nations that are always extending their borders but cannot retain their conquests.
French actress Sophie Arnold's comment on a fellow actress who was always losing work because she'd fall pregnant every year

She appears to be suffering from fallen archness.
Critic Franklin Pierce Adams on Helen Hayes' performance in George Bernard Shaw's **Caesar and Cleopatra**.

She's a great actress—from the waist down.
Sarah Bernhardt's comment on a colleague (which some sources also attribute to Dame Margaret Kendal about Sarah Bernhardt).

Radio is a bag of mediocrity where little men with cardboard minds wallow in the sluice of their own making.

Television is a device that permits people who haven't anything to do watch people who can't do anything.

You can take all the sincerity in Hollywood, place it in the navel of a fruit fly and still have room enough for three caraway seeds and a producer's heart.

Fred Allen

I have a previous engagement which I shall make as soon as possible.
John Barrymore getting out of a lunch he didn't want to have with a producer

O Calcutta! is the sort of show that gives pornography a bad name.
Clive Barnes

HEPBURN: Thank God I don't have to act with you anymore!
BARRYMORE: Oh, I didn't know you ever had.
Katharine Hepburn to John Barrymore, relieved to have finally finished filming
A Bill of Divorcement

Tallulah Bankhead

More of an act than an actress.
Anonymous comments on the US actress.

Tallulah Bankhead barged down the Nile last night as Cleopatra and sank.
Critic John Mason Brown, reviewing Shakespeare's **Anthony and Cleopatra**

Watching Tallulah on stage is like watching somebody skating on thin ice. Everyone wants to be there when it breaks.
Mrs Patrick Campbell

I'm as pure as the driven slush.
Tallulah Bankhead, describing herself

Elizabeth Taylor

Elizabeth Taylor looks like two small boys fighting underneath a thick blanket.
Fashion critic Richard Blackwell

She has an insipid double chin, her legs are too short, and she has a slight potbelly.
Richard Burton talking about Elizabeth Taylor, whom he later married—twice.

Every man should have the opportunity of sleeping with Elizabeth Taylor—and at the rate she's going everyone will.
Nicky Hilton, on his ex-wife

🖙 🖙 🖙

Cruise is a perfect example of a person who is simultaneously in love with and completely unfamiliar with himself, living in perpetual fear of self-actualization, and asserting a legal right to live free of criticism. A guy who can do whatever the hell he wants, yet chooses to devote his life to maintaining the public perception that he is somebody else.
Beast Magazine's description of Tom Cruise

More than just another insufferable Hollywood egotist, Oprah is something more akin to a housewife messiah, providing false hope and faux spirituality for experience-deprived worshippers. Everything she does is strategically designed to draw more praise, more devotees, and of course more money.
Beast Magazine's description of Oprah Winfrey

It opened at 8:40 sharp and closed at 10:40 dull.
Critic Heywood Broun on a forgotten production. On another occasion, when Broun reviewed actor Geoffrey Steyne he called the performance 'the worst to be seen in the contemporary theatre.' Steyne then did the totally amateurish thing and sued. Steyne lost the case. The next time he reviewed Steyne, Broun wrote that Steyne's performance was 'not up to his usual standard.'

He acts as if he's got a Mixmaster stuck up his ass and doesn't want anyone to know it.
Marlon Brando on Montgomery Clift

The famous and their professions

A fan club is a group of people who tell an actor that he is not alone in the way he feels about himself.
Jack Carson

Chevy Chase couldn't ad-lib a fart after a baked bean dinner.
Johnny Carson

I go to the theatre to be entertained. I don't want to see rape, sodomy, incest and drug addiction. I can get all that at home.
Peter Cook

Two things in the play should have been cut. The second act and that youngster's throat.
Noel Coward

Spielberg isn't a filmmaker. He's a confectioner.
UK film director Alex Cox on Steven Spielberg

Marilyn Monroe

There's a broad with her future behind her.
Constance Bennett on Marilyn Monroe

She was good at being inarticulately abstracted for the same reason that midgets are good at being short.
Clive James on Marilyn Monroe

Copulation was, I'm sure, Marilyn's uncomplicated way of saying thank you.
Nunnally Johnson on Marilyn Monroe

A vacuum with nipples.
Otto Preminger on Marilyn Monroe

She has breasts of granite and a mind like a Gruyere cheese.
Billy Wilder on Marilyn Monroe

Joan Collins

Joan Collins' career is a testimony to menopausal chic.
US writer Erica Jong

Joan Collins would sell her own bowel movements.
Ex-husband Anthony Newley

☙☙☙

Modesty is the artifice of actors, similar to passion in call girls.
Jackie Gleason

Any picture in which Errol Flynn is the best actor is its own worst enemy.
Ernest Hemingway

It's a new low for actresses when you have to wonder what's between her ears instead of her legs.
Katharine Hepburn on Sharon Stone

☙☙☙

Richard Briers last night played Hamlet like a demented typewriter.
WA. Darlington

Robert Mitchum does not so much act as point his suit at people.
Russell Davies

If laughter is contagious, my son has found the cure.
Les Dawson's mother

Glenda Jackson has a face to launch a thousand dredgers.
Jack de Manio

☙☙☙

A plumber's idea of Cleopatra.
W C Fields on Mae West

You always knew where you were with Sam Goldwyn. Nowhere.
F. Scott Fitzgerald

He's a male chauvinistic piglet.
Betty Friedan on Groucho Marx

What is *Uncle Vanya* about? I would say it is about as much as I can take.
Roger Garland

Lacks thrills, narrative, emotion, believability, character development, and, frankly, watchability.
Aaron Hillis on the movie Elektra

Devotees of awful filmmaking can't go wrong with this one.
Michael Wilmington on the movie Elektra

🍂 🍂 🍂

You had to stand in line to hate him.
US gossip columnist Hedda Hopper on US film producer Harry Cohn

An unreconstructed dinosaur.
US scriptwriter Budd Schulberg on Harry Cohn

🍂 🍂 🍂

Liza Minelli comes out looking like a giant rodent en route to a costume ball.
Stanley Kaufmann

Television—a medium. So called because it is neither rare nor well done.
Ernie Kovacs

When they asked Jack Benny to do something for the Actor's Orphanage—he shot both his parents and moved in.
Bob Hope talking about fellow comedian Jack Benny who was famous for his supposed stinginess.

Working with her was like being bombed by watermelons.
Alan Ladd on Sophia Loren

Not since Attila the Hun swept across Europe leaving 500 years of total blackness has there been a man like Lee Marvin.
Josh Logan

He has turned almost alarmingly blond—he's gone past platinum, he must be plutonium; his hair is coordinated with his teeth.

Film critic Pauline Kael on Robert Redford

Poor little man. They made him out of lemon Jell-O and there he is.

Adela Rogers St. Johns on Robert Redford

Doris Day is as wholesome as a bowl of cornflakes and at least as sexy.

Dwight MacDonald

If people don't sit at Chaplin's feet, he goes out and stands where they are sitting.

Hollywood screenwriter Herman J. Mankiewicz on Charlie Chaplin

Stephen Fry has all the wit of an unflushed toilet.

Bernard Manning

I didn't like the play, but then I saw it under adverse conditions—the curtain was up.

Groucho Marx

Hollywood is where the stars twinkle, then wrinkle.

Victor Mature

Waiting for Godot is a play in which nothing happens, twice.

Vivian Mercier

If she were cast as Lady Godiva, the horse would steal the show.

Patrick Murray

She ran the gamut of emotion from A to B.

Dorothy Parker on one of Katharine Hepburn's performances

Working with her is like being hit over the head with a valentine's card.

Christopher Plummer on Julie Andrews

Most of the time he sounds like he has a mouth full of toilet paper.

US movie critic Rex Reed talking about Marlon Brando

The famous and their professions

In Hollywood, if you don't have happiness, you send out for it.
Rex Reed

A woman went to a plastic surgeon and asked him to make her like Bo Derek. He gave her a lobotomy.
Joan Rivers

As entertaining as watching a potato bake.
US movie critic Marc Savlov on the movie **Taxi**

Sarah Brightman couldn't act scared on a New York subway at four o'clock in the morning.
Joel Segal

A fellow with the inventiveness of Albert Einstein but with the attention span of Daffy Duck.
US television critic Tom Shales on Robin Williams

☞ ☞ ☞

There are various versions of the following exchange between Irish playwright George Bernard Shaw and Winston Churchill. Here is the most succinct one:

SHAW: I am enclosing two tickets to the first night of my new play, bring a friend … if you have one.

CHURCHILL: Cannot possibly attend first night, will attend second … if there is one.

A tailor's advertisement making sentimental remarks to a milliner's advertisement in the middle of an upholsterer's and decorator's advertisement.

George Bernard Shaw on a particularly bad play. Note also this exchange with a critic who liked the performance of a couple of actors both he and Shaw were watching:

CRITIC: These men have been playing together for twelve years.
SHAW: Surely we've been here longer than that?

A freakish homunculus germinated outside lawful procreation.
Henry Jones on George Bernard Shaw

> Nature, not content with denying him the art of thinking, conferred on him the gift of writing.
> George Bernard Shaw

> Concerning no subject would Shaw be deterred by the minor accident of total ignorance from penning a definitive opinion.
> Roger Scruton

☞ ☞ ☞

An actress is someone with no ability who sits around waiting to go on alimony.
Jackie Stallone

In the first of these films, Miss Garland plays herself, which is horrifying; in the second someone else, which is impossible.
John Simon on Judy Garland

Charlotte Rampling—a poor actress who mistakes creepiness for sensuality.
John Simon

His voice is somewhere between bland and grandiose: blandiose perhaps.
Kenneth Tynan on Ralph Richardson

He's got a reputation as a great actor just by thinking hard about the next line.
King Vidor on Gary Cooper

If Woody Allen didn't exist then somebody would have knitted him.
Lesley White

The central problem of *Hamlet* is whether the critics are mad or only pretending to be mad.

The play was a great success, but the audience was a disaster.
Oscar Wilde

They shot too many pictures and not enough actors.
Walter Winchell

The famous and their professions

A steaming pile of clichés and screaming unlikelihoods.
US critic Jessica Winters on the movie **Hostage**

The characters are so flat and the dialogue so dull you expect it to be one of those movies whose existence is justified by a big final twist. But it's three days after the screening, and still no twist. Maybe it's coming in the mail?
Kyle Smith on the movie **The Jacket**

The play left a taste of lukewarm parsnip juice.

The scenery was beautiful—but the actors got in front of it.
Alexander Woollcott

Television: chewing gum for the eyes.
Frank Lloyd Wright

To me he is like a fly that tries to go out of a window and doesn't realise there is glass, and keeps banging against it, and never reaches the sky.
Franco Zeffirelli on fellow Italian film director Michelangelo Antonioni

Musicians, singers and dancers

We think of you every time we use a urinal.
Anonymous fans to South African musician PJ Powers who unwittingly took part in a poster campaign that feature mostly in public toilets. Powers later reportedly sued advertising agency McCann-Erikson for defamation for the humiliation she went through.

Modern music is three farts and a raspberry, orchestrated.
John Barbirolli

This boy will go far, when he has had less experience.
French composer Daniel-Francois-Esprit Auber's comment on the work of a young composer

The aesthetic equivalent of Vitamin D milk.
Beast Magazine's description of US singer Jessica Simpson

Anton Bruckner wrote the same symphony nine times (ten actually), trying to get it right. He failed.
Edward Abbey on Anton Bruckner

Riegger's *Dichotomy* sounded as though a pack of rats were being tortured to death, while from time to time, a dying cow moaned.
Walter Abendroth

She was a town-and-country soprano of the kind often used for augmenting grief at a funeral.
George Ade

⌇ ⌇ ⌇

Britney Spears has decided to crossover into country music. Now that she's a single mom with a deadbeat ex and a drinking problem, it seemed like a natural progression.
Anonymous

Boozy celebrity bimbos are replicating at an alarming rate these days, but the difference is this bilious tramp has two doomed children, both cursed with the warped ribonucleic helices of a beer-chugging swamp princess with a defective larynx and a lucky low-rent wannabe hustler who may actually be the more responsible parent.
Beast Magazine's description of Britney Spears and her ex Kevin Federline

⌇ ⌇ ⌇

I find that distance lends enchantment to bagpipes.
William Blezard

A violin is the revenge exacted on the intestines of a dead cat.
Ambrose Bierce

Critics can't even make music by rubbing their back legs together.
Mel Brooks

Disc-jockeys are electronic lice.
Anthony Burgess

We cannot expect you to be with us all the time, but perhaps you would be kind enough to keep in touch now and again.
Sir Thomas Beecham to an underperforming member of his orchestra

Other Beecham quotes:

A musicologist is a man who can read music but can't hear it.

A trombone is a quaint and antique drainage system applied to the face.

Brass bands are all very well in their place—outdoors and several miles away.

I have never heard any Stockhausen, but I do believe I have stepped in some.

Harpists spend half their life tuning and the other half playing out of tune.

The best instrument is the bagpipes. They sound exactly the same when you finish learning as when you start.

The harpsichord is a birdcage played with a toasting fork.

The harpsichord sounds like two skeletons copulating on a corrugated tin roof.

The organ at Winchester Cathedral is audible at five miles, painful at three and lethal at one.

The singers think that they are going to be heard. It is the duty of the orchestra to make sure that they are not.

Why do we have to have all these third-rate foreign conductors around—when we have so many second-rate ones of our own?

♥ ♥ ♥

I liked your opera. I think I will set it to music.
Ludwig van Beethoven to a fellow composer

Beethoven always sounds like the upsetting of bags with here and there a dropped hammer.
John Ruskin on Ludwig van Beethoven (1770-1827)

🖙🖙🖙

It is gaudy musical harlotry, savage and incoherent bellowings.
Boston Gazette on Franz Liszt

He writes the ugliest music extant.
Dramatic and Musical Review (1843) on Franz Liszt

Composition indeed! Decomposition is the proper word for such hateful fungi.
Dramatic and Musical World (1855) on Franz Liszt

Mick Jagger

I think Mick Jagger would be astounded and amazed if he realised how many people do not regard him as a sex symbol.
Angie Bowie

He moves like a parody between a majorette girl and Fred Astaire.

Mick Jagger is about as sexy as a pissing toad.
Truman Capote

Mick Jagger also came off second best in this exchange with jazz singer George Melly:

'I didn't expect you to have so many wrinkles,' Melly said.
'They're not wrinkles,' Jagger replied. 'They're laughter lines.'
'Really?' said Melly. 'Surely nothing could be that funny!'

Mick Jagger has big lips. I once saw him suck an egg out of a chicken.
Joan Rivers on Mick Jagger

🖙🖙🖙

The closest sound to Roseanne Barr's singing the National Anthem was my cat getting neutered.
Johnny Carson

The famous and their professions

... it is impossible to deny that his music is a soporific, by the side of which the telephone book is a strong cup of coffee.
Samuel Chotzinoff on Austrian composer Alban Berg

❧ ❧ ❧

The biggest no-talent I ever worked with.
US saxophonist Paul Cohen on Buddy Holly

Listening to the Fifth Symphony of Ralph Vaughan Williams is like staring at a cow for forty-five minutes.
Aaron Copland on Ralph Vaughan Williams

The tuba is certainly the most intestinal of instruments, the very lower bowel of music.
Peter de Vries

No-one can compete with McLaren when he is ranting like a highly strung washerwoman about his favourite subject: himself.
James Delingpole on Malcolm Mclaren

The third movement of Bartok's Fourth Quartet began with a dog howling at midnight, proceeded to imitate the regurgitations of the less-refined type of water closet and concluded with the cello reproducing the screech of an ungreased wheelbarrow.
Alan Dent

I don't like composers who think. It gets in the way of their plagiarism.
Howard Dietz

Bambi with testosterone.
Entertainment Weekly film critic Owen Gleiberman on Prince when he was The Artist Formerly Known As Prince

The Pogues have done for Irish music what Shane McGowan did for dentistry.
Roy Gullane

Shostakovich is without doubt the foremost composer of pornographic music in the history of art.
W J Henderson on Dmitri Shostakovich

The inventor of the bagpipes was inspired when he saw a man carrying an indignant asthmatic pig under his arm. Unfortunately, the manmade sound never equalled the purity of the sound achieved by the pig.

Alfred Hitchcock

The trouble with a lot of songs you hear nowadays is that somebody forgot to put them to music.

Sammy Kahn

Pianist and comedian Oscar Levant was as well known for his witticisms as his musicianship. When comedian Milton Berle became a Christian Scientist, Tonight Show host Jack Parr asked him for his comment. Levant replied, 'Our loss is their loss.' His comment on musicals in general is also typical: 'A series of catastrophes ending with a floor show.'

On the US conductor Leonard Bernstein:

His conducting has a masturbatory, oppressive and febrile zeal, even for the most tranquil passages. (Today he uses music as an accompaniment to his conducting.)

Leonard Bernstein is revealing musical secrets that have been common knowledge for centuries.

I think a lot of Leonard Bernstein—but not as much as he does.

On Doris Day:
I knew Doris Day before she was a virgin.

On Western movie actor and Roy Rogers sidekick Gabby Hayes:

Everyone in Hollywood is gay, except Gabby Hayes—and that's because he is a transvestite.

On Zsa Zsa Gabor:
She has discovered the secret of perpetual middle age.

On Dinah Shore:
The only person who ever left the Iron Curtain wearing it.

The famous and their professions

He's so worn by experience he has bags under his head.
Clive James on Charles Aznavour

The Sydney Opera House looks like a typewriter full of oyster shells, like a broken Pyrex casserole dish in a brown cardboard box.
Clive James

The Sydney Opera House looks as if it is something that has crawled out of the sea and is up to no good.
Beverley Nichols

Do we need a two-and-a-half hour movie about The Doors? I don't think so. I'll sum it up for you: I'M DRUNK—I'M FAMOUS—I'M DRUNK—I'M DEAD. *Big Fat Dead Guy in a Bathtub*, there's your title.
Comedian Denis Leary on the movie about Jim Morrison and The Doors

Jerry Lee Lewis has been married twenty times. He gets married on a Tuesday, they find his wife dead in a swimming pool on Thursday. Maybe if you married someone old enough to swim next time, OK Jerry?
Denis Leary

🖝 🖝 🖝

Art is long and life is short; here is evidently the explanation of a Brahms symphony.
Edward Lome on Johannes Brahms

I couldn't stand Janis Joplin's voice ... She was just a screaming little loudmouthed chick.
US musician Arthur Lee on Janis Joplin

He sounds like he's got a brick dangling from his willy, and a food mixer making puree of his tonsils.
Paul Lester on Jon Bon Jovi

He plays four-and-a-half-hour sets. That's torture. Does he hate his audience?
John Lydon on Bruce Springsteen

Why does Courtney Pine always look like a startled dildo?
Robert Mapplethorpe

You only notice a Tracy Chapman record when it ends, like a faint humming in your ear that has suddenly stopped.
Melody Maker magazine

The boy's got more plastic on him than a Co-Op bag.
Melody Maker on Michael Jackson

Michael Jackson's album was only called *Bad* because there wasn't enough room on the sleeve for *Pathetic*.
The Artist Formally Known as Prince

Michael Jackson looks like a Barbie doll that has been whittled by a malicious brother.
Thomas Sutcliffe

La Trina Turner—these days she's as tasty and hygienic as a mouthful of Domestos.
Melody Maker on Tina Turner

I could eat alphabet soup and shit better lyrics than that.
Johnny Mercer

Is he just doing a bad Elvis pout, or was he born that way?
Freddie Mercury on Billy Idol

Rock 'n' roll is musical baby food: it is the worship of mediocrity, brought about by a passion for conformity.
Mitch Miller

Going to the opera, like getting drunk, is a sin that carries its own punishment with it.
Hannah More

She is closer to organised prostitution than anything else.
Former lead singer of The Smiths, Morrissey, talking about Madonna

He sometimes brings out records with the greatest titles in the world, which somewhere along the line he neglects to write songs for.
Elvis Costello on Morrissey

The famous and their professions

I have my standards. They may be low, but I have them.
Bette Midler

Fauré writes the sort of music a pederast might hum while raping a choirboy.
Marcel Proust

Of course we've all dreamed of reviving the castrati and I have drawn up a list of well-known singers I'm sure would benefit. It's only a matter of getting them to agree.
Henry Reed

Actually, I never liked Dylan's kind of music before; I always thought he sounded just like Yogi Bear.
UK guitarist Mick Ronson on Bob Dylan

If he'd been making shell cases during the war it might have been better for music.
Camille Saint-Saëns on Maurice Ravel

It's bad when they don't perform your operas but when they do, it's far worse.
Camille Saint-Saëns on Dame Ethel Smyth

She would be like Richard Wagner if only she looked a bit more feminine.
Osbert Sitwell (1892-1969), poet and writer, on Dame Ethel Smyth

How is it possible for Bob Dylan to play the harmonica for thirty years and still show no sign of improvement?
Dave Sinclair

Too many pieces of music finish too long after the end.
Igor Stravinsky

I've seen Bauhaus, so I've seen bad, and I've seen Foreigner, so I've seen worse.
Steve Sutherland

If there is music in hell it will be bagpipes.
Joseph Tomelty

It's kind of like watching a chicken trying to fly, you wish it would stop, or turn into a swan, or even just stop trying so hard.
The Stud Brothers on Belinda Carlisle

The face that launched a thousand whores.
The Stud Brothers on Debbie Harry

After the United States premier of *Salome*, the critics went up into the attic and dusted off adjectives that hadn't been in use since Ibsen was first produced in London. I remember that 'bestial', 'fetid', 'slimy' and 'nauseous' were among the more complimentary terms.
Deems Taylor

The chief objection to playing wind instruments is that it prolongs the life of the player.

Dame Kiri Te Kanawa is a viable alternative to Valium.
Ira Siff

Jazz: Music invented by demons for the torture of imbeciles.
Henry Vandyke

Wagner

A composer for one right hand.
Richard Wagner on Frederic Chopin

I love Wagner, but the music I prefer is that of a cat hung up by its tail outside a window and trying to stick to the panes of glass with its claws.
Charles Baudelaire

The music of Wagner imposes mental tortures that only algebra has the right to inflict.
Paul de Saint-Victor

Wagner, thank the fates, is no hypocrite. He says what he means, and he usually means something nasty.
James Gibbons Huneker on Richard Wagner

Wagner is the Puccini of music.
JB Morton

Is Wagner actually a man? Is he not rather a disease? Everything he touches falls ill: he has made music sick.
Friedrich Nietzsche on Richard Wagner

Wagner was a monster. He was anti-Semitic on Mondays and vegetarian on Tuesdays. On Wednesday he was in favour of annexing Newfoundland, Thursday he wanted to sink Venice and Friday he wanted to blow up the Pope.
Tony Palmer on Richard Wagner

Parsifal is the kind of opera that starts at 6 o'clock. After it has been going on for six hours you look at your watch and it says 6:20.
David Randolf

Wagner has beautiful moments but awful quarter hours.
Gioachino Rossini on Richard Wagner

Wagner writes like an intoxified pig.
George T. Strong

I like Wagner's music better than any other music. It is so loud that one can talk the whole time without people hearing what one says. That is a great advantage.
Oscar Wilde on Richard Wagner

Wagner's music is better than it sounds.
Mark Twain on Richard Wagner

🖝 🖝 🖝

Mr Robin Day asks me to vouch for the fact that he can sing. I testify that the noise he makes is in fact something between that of a cat drowning, a lavatory flushing and a hyena devouring her afterbirth in the Appalachian Mountains under a full moon.
Auberon Waugh

He has Van Gogh's ear for music.
Billy Wilder

He is to piano playing as David Soul is to acting; he makes Jacques Loussier sound like Bach; he reminds us how cheap potent music can be.
Richard Williams on Richard Clayderman

Lloyd Webber's music is everywhere, but so is AIDS.
Malcolm Williamson

Most rock journalism is people who cannot write interviewing people who cannot talk for people who cannot read.
Frank Zappa

Painters, artists, architecture and the world of fashion

It takes forty dumb animals to make a fur coat, but only one to wear it.
Bryn Jones

A decorator tainted with insanity.
US critic Kenyon Cox on Paul Gauguin

Would have drowned the survivors on the Titanic and used their corpses as a human pontoon to walk to dry land.
Beast Magazine's description of Martha Stewart

Never in the history of fashion has so little material been raised so high to reveal so much that needs to be covered so badly.
Cecil Beaton on the miniskirt

A lot of people criticise supermodels and I think that's very unfair, because they can't answer back.
Jo Brand

Saint Laurent has excellent taste. The more he copies me, the better taste he displays.
Coco Chanel on Yves Saint Laurent

It makes me look as if I were straining a stool.
Winston Churchill commenting on his famous portrait by Graham Sutherland

Abstract art? A product of the untalented, sold by the unprincipled to the utterly bewildered.
Al Capp

A head so empty, the rails of coke that sustain her must dissipate in clouds around her ears; this residual high the only explanation anyone would come within five feet of her. Brainless, her spinal cord defies physics, like an Indian rope trick.
Beast Magazine's description of Paris Hilton

Modern Art is what happens when painters stop looking at girls and persuade themselves they have a better idea.
John Ciardi

In the flesh Cindy Crawford is, inevitably, more plastic than perfect. Like her Hambro namesake, she seems so plastic and perfect that I had this insatiable urge to pull down her trousers to see if she had any reproductive organs.
British journalist Nicola Davison

The art galleries of Paris contain the finest collection of frames I ever saw.
Humphry Davy

The world's worst piece of art is reputed to be *Le Remede* by Antoine Watteau. It depicts a reclining Venus about to receive an enema administered by her chambermaid.
Bruce Felton

When having my portrait painted I don't want justice, I want mercy.
Billy Hughes

Jeff Koon's work is the last bit of methane left in the intestine of the dead cow that is postmodernism.
Robert Hughes

It is only too easy to catch people's attention by doing something worse than anyone else has dared to do it before.
From an article in Le Charivari (an illustrated Parisian Newspaper published between 1832 and 1937) on Claude Monet

***

You ask me, sir, for a suitable institution to which you propose to leave your paintings. May I suggest an asylum for the blind?
James McNeill Whistler

My dear Whistler, you leave your pictures in such a sketchy, unfinished state. Why don't you ever finish them?
UK painter Frederic Leighton on James McNeill Whistler

My dear Leighton, why do you ever begin yours?
James McNeill Whistler on Frederic Leighton

Whistler once made a particularly witty remark at a dinner that Oscar Wilde was also attending:

'I wish I had said that!' said Wilde.
'You will, Oscar, you will,' said Whistler.
In fact, as you've probably guessed, the civilised feud between Whistler and Wilde was only one of many that Whistler had.

The only thoroughly original ideas I have ever heard Mr Whistler express have had reference to his own superiority as a painter over painters greater than himself.
Oscar Wilde

***

If it sells, it's art.
Frank Lloyd Wright

Who among us has not gazed at a painting of Jackson Pollock and not thought 'What a piece of crap'?
Rob Long

Who is this chap Augustus John? He drinks, he's dirty and I know there are women in the background.
Bernard Montgomery

The only genius with an IQ of 60.
Gore Vidal talking about Andy Warhol

The famous and their professions

An enraged cartoonist burst into the office of the editor of the *New Yorker* and shouted, 'You never use my stuff but you publish the work of a fifth-rate artist like Thurber.' The editor immediately sprang to my defense. 'Third-rate,' he said.
James Thurber

Writers, poets and journalists

You can get away with saying anything stupid, as long as you attribute it to Samuel Johnson, Marcus Aurelius or Dorothy Parker.
George Mikes

Mr Alfred Austin has a clearly-defined talent, the limits of which are by this time generally recognised.
Anonymous insult to the British Poet Laureate

A one-man slum.
Anonymous description of US journalist Heywood Campbell Broun. Perhaps this opinion came about because of exchanges like this—

US CONGRESSMAN ABOUT TO BE INTERVIEWED BY BROUN:
    I have nothing to say, young man.

BROUN: I know. Now shall we get on with the interview?

There is nothing as rare as a Woollcott first edition except perhaps a second edition.
Franklin P. Adams

This is one of those big, fat paperbacks, intended to while away a monsoon or two, which, if thrown with a good overarm action, will bring a water buffalo to its knees.
Nancy Banks-Smith reviewing MM Kaye's The Far Pavilions

That old yahoo George Moore. His stories impressed me as being on the whole like gruel spooned off a dirty floor.
Jane Barlow

Chopra's work proves only one thing: he's just another mystical moron providing a psychic security blanket to soft-skulled suckers.
Beast Magazine's description of Deepak Chopra

It only makes sense that an infantile, semiliterate, cliché-humping fabulist would become a best-selling author in a country that only reads books to keep Oprah off its back. ... Frey's success is just another sign that people will believe anything, so long as it makes them feel good and doesn't challenge them intellectually.
Beast Magazine's description of James 'A Million Little Pieces' Frey

It's hard to believe this repulsive shit fountain is even human, until you remember that we share 70% of our DNA with pigs.
Beast Magazine's description of Rush Limbaugh

The kind of jerk that'd steer a tour bus off a cliff, then charge every passenger 20 bucks to hear him scream, "We're all going to die!"
Beast Magazine's description of Bob Woodward (of Watergate fame)

Robert Bridge's anthology, *The Spirit of Man*, is like a vomit after a rich meal.
AC Benson

🖋 🖋 🖋

Shaw, you ought to be roasted alive, though even then, you would not be to my taste.
James Barrie to George Bernard Shaw

I would cheerfully pay George Bernard Shaw's funeral expenses at any time.
Henry Irving

George Bernard Shaw writes like a Pakistani who has learned English when he was twelve years old to become a chartered accountant.
John Osborne

The covers of this book are too far apart.
Ambrose Bierce

The stupid person's idea of a clever person.
Anglo-Irish novelist Elizabeth Bowen on Aldous Huxley

Henry Miller is not really a writer but a non-stop talker to whom someone has given a typewriter.
Gerald Brenan

❦ ❦ ❦

The same old sausage, fizzing and sputtering in its own grease.
Henry James on Thomas Carlyle

We did not conceive it possible that even Mr Lincoln would produce a paper so slipshod, so loose-joined, so puerile, not alone in literary construction, but in its ideas, its sentiments, its grasp. He has outdone himself.
Chicago Times on Abraham Lincoln's Gettysburg Address (19 November 1863)

If you put two economists in a room, you get two opinions, unless one of them is Keynes, in which case you get three opinions.
Winston Churchill

This is a book that everyone can afford to be without.
Edmund Crispin

❦ ❦ ❦

Jeffrey Archer is proof of the proposition that in each of us there lurks a bad novel.
Julian Critchley

Last time I was in Spain I got through six Jeffrey Archer novels. I must remember to bring enough toilet paper next time.
Bob Monkhouse

❦ ❦ ❦

His books are going like wildfire. Everybody is burning them.
George DeWitt

I am sorry to hear you are going to publish a poem. Can't you suppress it?
Elizabeth, Lady Holland, to Lord Porchester

Immature poets imitate. Mature poets steal.
TS Eliot

❦ ❦ ❦

He has never been known to use a word that might send a reader
to the dictionary.
William Faulkner on Ernest Hemingway

Poor Faulkner. Does he really think big emotions come from big
words?
Ernest Hemingway on William Faulkner

Always willing to lend a helping hand to the one above him.
F. Scott Fitzgerald on Ernest Hemingway

❦ ❦ ❦

George Sand was a great cow-full of ink.
Gustave Flaubert

An editor should have a pimp for a brother so he'd have someone
to look up to.
Gene Fowler

Thank you for sending me a copy of your book—I'll waste no time
reading it.
Moses Hadas

Jack Anderson is the lowest form of human being to walk the earth.
He's a muckraker who lies, steals and let me tell you this ... he'll go
lower than dog shit for a story.
FBI Director J. Edgar Hoover on US investigative journalist Jack Anderson

As a work of art it has the same status as a long conversation
between two not very bright drunks.
Clive James on **Princess Daisy** by Judith Krantz

Donne's verses are like the peace and mercy of God. Like His peace,
they pass all understanding, and like His mercy they seem to endure
forever.
King James I on poet John Donne

***

You have but two topics, yourself and me and I'm sick of both.
Samuel Johnson to his biographer James Boswell

Paradise Lost is a book that, once put down, is very hard to pick up again.
Samuel Johnson on John Milton's famous epic poem

***

James, why don't you write books that people can read?
Nora Joyce to her husband

In Ireland they try to make a cat clean by rubbing its nose in its own filth. James Joyce has tried the same treatment on the human subject. I hope it may prove successful.
George Bernard Shaw

***

A good many young writers make the mistake of enclosing a stamped, self-addressed envelope, big enough to send a manuscript back in. This is too much temptation for the editor.
Ring Lardner

Every good journalist has a novel in him—which is an excellent place for it.
Russell Lynes

It was a book to kill time for those who like it better dead.
Rose Macaulay

That writer is so bad he shouldn't be left alone with a typewriter.
Herman J. Manciewicz

If you want to get rich from writing, write the sort of thing that's read by persons who move their lips when they're reading to themselves.
Don Marquis

From the moment I picked your book up until I laid it down I was convulsed with laughter. Some day I intend reading it.
Groucho Marx

Every word that Lillian Hellman writes is a lie, including 'and' and 'the'.
Mary McCarthy

One day we shall strangle the last publisher with the entrails of the last literary agent.
David Mercer

GK Chesterton and Hilaire Belloc were the two buttocks of one bum.
T. Sturge Moore

Though he tortures the English language, he has never yet succeeded in forcing it to reveal its meaning.
JB Morton

Writers of thrillers tend to gravitate to the Secret Service as the mentally unstable become psychiatrists and the impotent become pornographers.
Malcolm Muggeridge

A huge pendulum attached to a small clock.
Russian critic Ivan Panin on Samuel Taylor Coleridge

This is not a book that should be tossed lightly aside. It should be hurled with great force.
Dorothy Parker on Benito Mussolini's novel **Claudia Particella**

Thomas the Wank Engine.
Private Eye's description of DM Thomas' Memories and **Hallucinations**

Dorothy Thompson is the only woman who had her menopause in public and got paid for it.
Alice Roosevelt (Actually this isn't true. Germaine Greer also comes to mind.)

No self-respecting dead fish would want to be wrapped in a Murdoch newspaper, let alone work for it.
George Royko

🌂 🌂 🌂

I have often wished I had time to cultivate modesty, but I am too busy thinking about myself.
Edith Sitwell

Virginia Woolf's writing is no more than glamorous knitting. I believe she must have a pattern somewhere.
Edith Sitwell

Edith Sitwell's interest in art was largely confined to portraits of herself.
John Fowles

🐛 🐛 🐛

Thomas Gray walks as if he had fouled his small clothes, and looks as if he smelt it.
Christopher Smart

In conversation he is even duller than in writing, if that is possible.
Juliana Smith on lexicographer Noah Webster

Poor Matthew Arnold, he's gone to heaven no doubt—but he won't like God.
Robert Louis Stevenson

You don't really want to be a poet. First of all, if you're a woman, you have to be three times better than all of the men. Second, you have to fuck everyone. Thirdly, you have to be dead.
US poet Mark Strand to an aspiring poetess

Steele might become a reasonably good writer if he would pay a little more attention to grammar, learn something about the propriety and disposition of words and, incidentally, get some information on the subject he intends to handle.
Jonathan Swift

My brother-in-law wrote an unusual murder story. The victim got killed by a man from another book.
Robert Sylvester

Somebody's boring me. I think it's me.
Dylan Thomas

Mr Waugh is a parochial English writer (tautologies gush from my pen!)
Gore Vidal

He is every other inch a gentleman.
Rebecca West on Michael Arlen

🖝 🖝 🖝

Sir Lewis Morris complained to Oscar Wilde about the lack of support he was getting for the nomination of Poet Laureate:
'There is a conspiracy of silence against me! A conspiracy of silence! What should I do, Oscar?'
'Join it,' said Wilde.

Other Wildean literary stings:

George Moore leads his readers into the latrine and locks them in.

George Moore wrote excellent English until he discovered grammar.

One should not be too severe on English novels; they are the only relaxation of the intellectually unemployed.

The difference between journalism and literature is that journalism is unreadable and literature is never read.

There is much to be said in favour of modern literary journalism. By giving us the opinions of the uneducated, it keeps us in touch with the ignorance of the community.

Oscar Wilde paraphrased and inverted the witticisms of others. His method of literary piracy was on the lines of the robber Cacus, who dragged stolen cows backwards by the tails to his cavern so that their hoof prints might not lead to detection.
George Moore

Critics

Reviewers ... seemed to fall into two classes: those who had little to say, and those that had nothing.
British writer Max Beerbohm

Taking to pieces is the trade of those who cannot construct.
US poet Ralph Waldo Emerson

A critic is a man created to praise greater men than himself, but he is never able to find them.
UK playwright Richard Le Gallienne

Nature fits all her children with something to do. He who would write and can't write would surely review, can set up a small booth as a critic, and sell the US his petty conceit and his pettier jealousies.
US poet James Lowell

Criticism is prejudice made plausible.
US critic H L Mencken

A critic is a legless man who teaches running.
US writer Channing Pollock

I am sitting in the smallest room in the house. I have your review in front of me. Soon it will be behind me.
Max Reger

A dramatic critic is a man who leaves no turn unstoned.
George Bernard Shaw

As a bankrupt thief turns thief-taker, so an unsuccessful author turns critic.
Percy Bysshe Shelley

2. Stupidity, dullness, ignorance, laziness, pomposity, pettiness, stinginess, mediocrity and incompetence

If all else fails, immortality can always be assured by a spectacular error.
JK Galbraith

He may look like an idiot and talk like an idiot but don't let that fool you. He really is an idiot.
Groucho Marx

Most beautiful dumb girls think they are smart and get away with it because other people, on the whole, aren't much smarter.
Louise Brooks

His mind is so open—so open that ideas simply pass through it.
British philosopher FH Bradley on a colleague

Stay with me; I want to be alone.
Joey Adams

What's on your mind? If you'll forgive the overstatement.
US comedian Fred Allen

My problems all started with my early education. I went to a school for mentally disturbed teachers.
Woody Allen

Your head is as empty as a eunuch's underpants.
Rowan Atkinson as Blackadder

If a man is a fool, you don't train him out of being a fool by sending him to university. You merely turn him into a trained fool, ten times more dangerous.
Desmond Bagley

Dublin University contains the cream of Ireland—rich and thick.
Samuel Beckett

So boring you fall asleep halfway through her name.
Alan Bennett

End of season sale at the cerebral department.
Gareth Blackstock

He's so tight that if you stuck a piece of coal up his ass, in two weeks you'd have a diamond.
Matthew Broderick as Ferris Bueller.

He was so thick he couldn't tell which way a lift was going if he got two guesses.
Roy Brown

He was born stupid, and greatly increased his birthright.
Samuel Butler

She's got such a narrow mind, when she walks fast her earrings bang together.
John Cantu

Differently clued.
Dave Clark

Never attribute to malice that which can be adequately explained by straightforward stupidity.
JC Collins

Little things affect little minds.
Benjamin Disraeli

He can barely read and write—Eton of course.
Lawrence Durrell

I'm about as useful as a one-legged man at an arse-kicking contest.
Dave Dutton

His ignorance is encyclopaedic.
Abba Eban

Only two things are infinite, the universe and human stupidity, and I'm not sure about the former.
Albert Einstein

Harvard is a storehouse of knowledge because the freshmen bring so much in and the graduated take so little out.
Charles W. Eliot

Before I came here I was confused about this subject. Having listened to you lecture, I am still confused. But on a higher level.
Enrico Fermi

Ordinarily he is insane. But he has lucid moments when he is only stupid.
Heinrich Heine

Some men are born mediocre, some men achieve mediocrity, and some men have mediocrity thrust upon them.
Joseph Heller

Some people stay longer in an hour than others can in a week.
William Dean Howells

Some folks seem to have descended from the chimpanzee later than others.
Kin Hubbard

God was bored by him.
Victor Hugo

He was so narrow-minded he could see through a keyhole with both eyes.
Molly Ivins

Stupidity, dullness, ignorance, laziness ...

Next-day delivery in a nanosecond world.
Van Jacobson

He is not only dull himself, he is the cause of dullness in others.

He had delusions of adequacy.
Walter Kerr

He was one of those men who possess almost every gift, except the gift of the power to use them.
Charles Kingsley

The private papers that Herbert Morrison left behind were so dull and banal that they would provide illumination only if they were burned.
Greg Knight

If he ever had a bright idea it would be beginner's luck.
William Lashner

Sharp as a sack full of wet mice.
Looney Tunes rooster Foghorn Leghorn

I wish I'd known you when you were alive.
Leonard Louis Levinson

He can compress the most words into the smallest idea of any man I know.
Abraham Lincoln

You've got the brain of a four-year-old boy, and I bet he was glad to get rid of it.
Groucho Marx

She had a pretty gift for quotation, which is a serviceable substitute for wit.

She plunged into a sea of platitudes, and with the powerful breast stroke of a channel swimmer, made her confident way towards the white cliffs of the obvious.
W. Somerset Maugham

When you go to the mind reader, do you get half price?

You look into his eyes, and you get the feeling someone else is driving.
David Letterman

I would not want to put him in charge of snake control in Ireland.
Eugene McCarthy

His mind is a muskeg of mediocrity.
Canadian writer John McNaughton on an unnamed university professor

Don't stand around doing nothing. People will think you're just a workman.
Spike Milligan

Yesterday was the first day of the rest of your life and you messed it up again.
Patrick Murray

I have been described as 'a lighthouse in the middle of a bog,' brilliant but useless.
Conor Cruise O'Brien

'I really can't come to your party, I can't bear fools,' a woman told Dorothy Parker.

'That's strange, your mother could,' she replied.

☞ ☞ ☞

Grammar schools are public schools without the sodomy.
Tony Parsons

I can't believe that out of 100,000 sperm, you were the quickest.
Steven Pearl

He has the attention span of a lightning bolt.
Robert Redford

Useless as a pulled tooth.
Mary Roberts Rinehart

Stupidity, dullness, ignorance, laziness ...

They never open their mouths without subtracting from the sum of human knowledge.
Thomas Brackett Reed

He never said a foolish thing nor never did a wise one.
Earl of Rochester

There is nothing as stupid as an educated man, if you get him off the subject he was educated in.
Will Rogers

Anyone who gives a surgeon six thousand dollars for a breast augmentation should give some thought to investing a little more in brain augmentation.
Mike Royko

The power of accurate observation is commonly called cynicism by those who have not got it.

The trouble with her is that she lacks the power of conversation but not the power of speech.
George Bernard Shaw

Consider also this comment by Israel Zangwill on George Bernard Shaw:
The way George Bernard Shaw believes in himself is very refreshing in these atheistic days when so many people believe in no God at all.

Forgotten insulter to British clergyman Sydney Smith:
'If I had a son who was an idiot, I would make him a parson.'
'Your father was evidently of a different opinion,' said Smith.

He not only overflowed with learning, but stood in the slop.
Sydney Smith

He is so stupid you can't trust him with an idea.
John Steinbeck

Trinity College Cambridge is like a dead body in a high state of putrefaction. The only interest is the worms that come out of it.
Lytton Strachey

While he was not dumber than an ox he was not any smarter either.
James Thurber

Teflon brain.
Lily Tomlin

The founding fathers in their wisdom decided that children were an unnatural strain on parents. So they provided jails called schools, equipped with torture called education.
John Updike

A great many people now reading and writing would be better employed keeping rabbits.
Edith Sitwell

Nannie was a devout Christian Scientist, but not a good one. She kept confusing herself with God. She didn't know when to step aside and give God a chance.
UK Socialite Mrs Gordon Smith on Nancy Astor

Anyone who has been to an English public school will always feel comparatively at home in prison.
Evelyn Waugh

A mental midget with the IQ of a fence post.
Tom Waits

She never lets ideas interrupt the easy flow of her conversation.
Jean Webster

Only dull people are brilliant at breakfast.
Oscar Wilde

No shirt is too young to be stuffed.
Larry Zolf on fellow Canadian politician Joe Clark

Stupidity, dullness, ignorance, laziness ...

Insults and put downs for the stupid

A half-wit gave you a piece of his mind, and you held on to it.

Ahhh ... I see the screw-up fairy has visited us again.

And there he was: reigning supreme at number two.

Any connection between your reality and mine is purely coincidental.

Are you a moron, or are you possessed by a retarded ghost?

Are you always so stupid or is today a special occasion?

Are you always this stupid or are you making a special effort today?

Brains aren't everything. In fact in your case they're nothing.

Don't let you mind wander—it's far too small to be let out on its own.

Calling you an idiot would be an insult to all the stupid people.

The closest he'll ever get to a brainstorm is a slight drizzle.

Did the mental hospital test too many drugs on you today?

Did your sideshow leave town without you?

Do you ever wonder what life would be like if you'd had enough oxygen at birth?

Doesn't know the meaning of the word fear, but then again he doesn't know the meaning of most words.

Don't get lost in thought; you'll be a total stranger there.

Don't say things like that; it just makes you sound stupid. In fact, don't talk at all. It just makes you sound stupid.

For two cents I'd give you a piece of my mind and all of yours.

Forgot to pay his brain bill.

Go ahead, tell them everything you know. It'll only take 10 seconds.

Have you considered suing your brains for non-support?

He got fired from the M&M factory for throwing away all the W's.

He got hit by a parked car.

He has one brain cell, and it is fighting for dominance.

He is always lost in thought—it's unfamiliar territory.

He is depriving a village somewhere of an idiot.

He is the kind of a man that you would use as a blueprint to build an idiot.

He sold the car for petrol money.

He tried to drop acid but the car battery fell on his foot.

Here's a flashlight so that you can pipe some light in to where your brains are located.

He's so dense that light bends around him.

His brain waves fall a little short of the beach.

How many years did it take you to learn how to breathe?

I don't think you are a fool, but what's my opinion compared to that of thousands of others.

I don't know what makes you so stupid, but it really works!

I enjoy talking to you, my mind needs a rest.

I hear you changed your mind! What did you do with the nappy?

I heard you got a brain transplant and the brain rejected you!

I hope you live to be as old as your jokes.

I like you. You remind me of when I was young and stupid.

I wish I had a lower IQ , so that I could enjoy your company.

I'd explain it to you, but I don't have any crayons with me.

I'd like to break the monotony; where's your weakest point?

If brains were taxed, you'd get a rebate.

I'd like to leave you with one thought ... but I'm not sure you have a place to put it!

If ignorance is bliss, you must be orgasmic.

If you ever tax your brain, don't charge more than a penny.

If you give him a penny for his thoughts, you get change back.

If you stand close enough to him, you can hear the ocean.

If you were any more stupid, you'd have to be watered twice a week.

If your IQ were any lower, you'd trip over it.

Ignorance can be cured. Stupidity is forever.

I'll try being nicer if you'll try being smarter.

I'm glad to see you're not letting your education get in the way of your ignorance.

Some drink from the fountain of knowledge; you only gargled.

Some people don't hesitate to speak their minds because they have nothing to lose.

You must have a sixth sense. There's no sign of the other five.

You sound reasonable ... time to up the medication.

You'd think that such a tiny mind would be lonely in such a big head.

You're having delusions of competence.

Your teeth are brighter than you are.

You're a person of rare intelligence; it's rare when you show any.

A collection of ways to call someone stupid

A few beers short of a six pack.

A few clowns short of a circus.

A few fries short of a Happy Meal.

All foam, no beer.

An experiment in artificial stupidity.

An intellect rivalled only by garden tools.

Couldn't pour water out of a boot with instructions on the heel.

Doesn't have all her cornflakes in one box.

Doesn't know much but leads the league in nostril hair.

Dumber than a box of hair.

Elevator doesn't go all the way to the top floor.

His antenna doesn't pick up all the channels.

Not the sharpest knife in the drawer.

One Fruit Loop shy of a full bowl.

Proof that evolution CAN go in reverse.

The lights are on, but nobody's home.

The wheel's spinning, but the mouse is dead.

3. Character assassination

In the old days insulting someone's ancestry was more fashionable than today. Although these sorts of attacks still have some life in them, perhaps nowadays, in an age where people value success and popularity or style over substance, the worst thing you can say about a person is how much of a loser or how hated they are. It all depends on their insecurities.

• • • • • • •

He is mad, bad and dangerous to know.
Lady Caroline Lamb's famous description of Lord Byron

He hasn't an enemy in the world—but all his friends hate him.
Eddie Cantor no doubt inspired by Oscar Wilde's similar, 'He has no enemies, but is intensely disliked by his friends.'

He's so small, he's a waste of skin.

He was so narrow-minded that if he fell on a pin it would blind him in both eyes.
Fred Allen

I'd call him a sadistic, hippophilic necrophile, but that would be beating a dead horse.
Woody Allen

If your parents got a divorce would they still be brother and sister?

You're obviously from the shallow end of the gene pool.
Anonymous

Why are we honouring this man? Have we run out of human beings?
Milton Berle

She not only expects the worst, but makes the worst of it when it happens.
Michael Arlen

Too intense contemplation of his own genius had begun to undermine his health.
Max Beerbohm

Sara could commit adultery at one end and weep for her sins at the other, and enjoy both operations at once.
Joyce Cary

She was the kind of girl who'd eat all your cashews and leave you with nothing but peanuts and filberts.
Raymond Chandler

I see her as one great stampede of lips directed at the nearest derrière.

She had much in common with Hitler, only no moustache.
Noël Coward

I was actually the first birth from an inflatable woman.
Tony de Meur

May I suggest, sir, that if you want an impenetrable disguise for the fancy dress ball, that you go sober?
Samuel Foote

I thought men like that shot themselves.
King George V

He has sat on the fence so long that the iron has entered his soul.
David Lloyd George

Noone can have a higher opinion of him than I have; and I think he's a dirty little beast.
WS Gilbert

The best part of you ran down your mother's legs.
Jackie Gleason

He once had his toes amputated so that he could stand closer to the bar.
Mike Harding

He was so crooked that when he died, they had to screw him into the ground.
Bob Hope

Her only flair is in her nostrils.
Pauline Kael

He is simply a shiver looking for a spine to run up.
Paul Keating

She looked as though butter wouldn't melt in her mouth—or anywhere else.
Elsa Lanchester

She's descended from a long line her mother listened to.
Gypsy Rose Lee

She could carry off anything; and some people said that she did.
Ada Leverson

She's the sort of woman who lives for others—you can tell the others by their hunted expression.
CS Lewis

Where others have hearts, he carries a tumour of rotten principles.
Jack London

I'll bet your father spent the first year of your life throwing rocks at the stork.

You're a good example of why some animals eat their children.
Groucho Marx

His face was filled with broken commandments.
John Masefield

He's liked, but he's not well liked.
Arthur Miller

He is one of those people who would be enormously improved by death.
HH Munro

She proceeds to dip her little fountain-pen filler into pots of oily venom and to squirt the mixture at all her friends.
Harold Nicholson

Even if your father had spent more of your mother's immoral earnings on your education you would not be a gentleman.
Frank Otter

You have a good and kind soul. It just doesn't match the rest of you.
Norm Papernick

The affair between Margot Asquith and Margot Asquith will live as one of the prettiest love stories in all literature.
Dorothy Parker

You're a parasite for sore eyes.
Gregory Ratoff

If you ever become a mother, can I have one of the puppies?
Charles Pierce

He thinks by infection, catching an opinion like a cold.
John Ruskin

Ooo, she's so cold, sweetie! I'll just bet she has her period in cubes.
Jennifer Saunders

He had a winning smile, but everything else was a loser.
George C. Scott

He never bore a grudge against anyone he wronged.
Simone Signoret

She is a water bug on the surface of life.
Gloria Steinem

She is such a good friend that she would throw all her acquaintances into the water for the pleasure of fishing them out again.
Charles Talleyrand on the French writer Mme de Stael

He was as great as a man can be without morality.
Alexis de Tocqueville

They don't hardly make 'em like him any more—but just to be on the safe side, he should be castrated anyway.
Hunter S. Thompson

He never chooses an opinion; he just wears whatever happens to be in style.
Leo Tolstoy

She never was really charming till she died.
Terence

He will lie even when it is inconvenient, the sign of a true artist.
Gore Vidal

No more sense of direction than a bunch of firecrackers.
Rob Wagner

He's the kind of man who picks his friends—to pieces.

His mother should have thrown him away and kept the stork.
Mae West

He would stab his best friend for the sake of writing an epigram on his tombstone.

He hasn't a single redeeming vice.
Oscar Wilde

He made enemies as naturally as soap makes suds.
Percival Wilde

I've got a friend who is a procrastinator. He didn't get a birthmark until he was eight years old.
Steven Wright

Character assassination

Character insults

At least you are not obnoxious like so many other people. You're obnoxious in a new and different way!

He has depth, but only on the surface. Down deep inside, he is shallow.

He was a bit like a corkscrew. Twisted, cold and sharp.
Kate Cruise O'Brien

His lack of education is more than compensated for by his keenly developed moral bankruptcy.
Woody Allen

He was so crooked, you could have used his spine for a safety-pin.
Dorothy L. Sayers

He'd steal the straw from his mother's kennel.

His personality's split so many ways he goes alone for group therapy.

I can tell you are lying. Your lips are moving.

I don't know anything about this man. Anyhow, I only know two things about him. One is, he has never been in jail, and the other is, I don't know why.
Mark Twain

I'm not your type. I'm not inflatable.

Have I met you someplace before? I sometimes get careless where I go.

Let's play horse. I'll be the front end and you be yourself.

You are so dishonest that I can't even be sure that what you tell me are lies!

You have delusions of adequacy.

You have more faces than a clock factory.

You should do some soul-searching. Maybe you'll find one.

You used to be arrogant and obnoxious. Now you are just the opposite. You are obnoxious and arrogant.

You're not yourself today. I noticed the improvement immediately.

You've given me something to live for—revenge.

You've got a great personality, but not for a human being.

You've got your head so far up your arse you can chew your food twice.

You've got your head so far up your arse I bet that you can see through your mouth.

Insults and put downs about ancestry

After meeting you, I've decided I am in favour of abortion in cases of incest.

All of your ancestors must number in the millions; it's hard to believe that many people are to blame for producing you.

All that you are you owe to your parents. Why don't you send them a penny and square the account?

Did your parents have any children that lived?

Ever since I saw your family tree I've wanted to cut it down.

His origins are so low, you'd have to limbo under his family tree.

I wish your parents had never met.

The overwhelming power of the sex drive was demonstrated by the fact that someone was willing to father you.

They should have thrown you away and christened the placenta.

You should be the poster child for birth control.

You were born because your mother didn't believe in abortion; now she believes in infanticide.

You're the sap in the family tree.

You're the load your mother should've swallowed.

Who pissed in your gene pool?

4. Looks and ageing

Vanity is always fun to insult and if there's one thing that people are vain about it's their personal appearance. So if you really want to hurt someone's feelings go for the looks, especially in the area of those great taboos of modern life—fat and ageing. As US journalist Helen Rowland said: The chief excitement in a woman's life is spotting women who are fatter than she is. Unsurprisingly, there are very few insults directed at being young or thin.

· · · · · · ·

Why grow around your face what grows naturally around your arse?
Anonymous comment on beards

My wife asked what it would take to make her look good. I said, 'about a mile'.
Anonymous

Queen Charlotte Sophia, consort to Britain's George III was never considered even remotely attractive, but her appearance improved marginally as she got older, prompting her chamberlain to remark that:
Yes, indeed. The bloom of her ugliness is going off.

These days he just exhausts himself grappling with temptation.
Anonymous

A face like a wedding cake left out in the rain.
Anonymous comment on UK poet WH Auden

Her hat is a creation that will never go out of style. It will look ridiculous year after year.
Fred Allen

She was really a bad-looking girl. Facially, she resembled Louis Armstrong's voice.
Woody Allen

She spends her day powdering her face till she looks like a bled pig.
Margot Asquith

She was a large woman who seemed not so much dressed as upholstered.
JM Barrie

Looks like a camel in drag.
Beast Magazine's description of US non-celebrity Nancy Grace

He was as ugly as a gargoyle hewn by a drunken stonemason for the adornment of a Methodist Chapel in one of the vilest suburbs of Leeds or Wigan.
Max Beerbohm

She was what we used to call a suicide blonde—dyed by her own hand.
US writer Saul Bellow

When I was a boy, the Dead Sea was only sick.
George Burns

A blank, helpless sort of face, rather like a rose just before you drench it with DDT.
UK academic John Carey on socialite Diana Cooper

Her skin was white as leprosy.
Samuel Taylor Coleridge

Pushing forty? She's hanging on for dear life.
UK novelist Ivy Compton-Burnett

His smile is like the silver plate on a coffin.
Irish lawyer John Philpott Curran

He is so old that his blood type was discontinued.
Bill Dana

When I go to the dentist, he's the one that has to have the anaesthetic.
Phyllis Diller

I got thrown out of Alcoholics Anonymous because when the other clients saw me they thought they were having the DTs.
Dave Dutton

Bertrand Russell looked like a vegetarian vulture.
AA Gill

He must have had a magnificent build before his stomach went in for a career of its own.
Margaret Halsey

She resembles the Venus de Milo: she is very old, has no teeth, and has white spots on her yellow skin.
Heinrich Heine

Her face was her chaperone.
Rupert Hughes

I have everything I had twenty years ago—except that now it's all lower.
Gypsy Rose Lee

Though I yield to no one in my admiration for Mr Coolidge, I do wish he did not look as if he had been weaned on a pickle.
US socialite Alice Roosevelt Longworth on Calvin Coolidge. Longworth also once said to a fellow guest at a dinner party: 'If you can't say anything good about someone, sit right here beside me.'

At first I thought he was walking a dog. Then I realized it was his date.
Edith Massey in **Polyester**

I never forget a face, but in your case I'll make an exception.

She got her good looks from her father. He's a plastic surgeon.
Groucho Marx

He's a trellis for varicose veins.
US playwright Wilson Mizner

He looked, I decided, like a letter delivered to the wrong address.
Malcolm Muggeridge on Evelyn Waugh

Guy Burgess had the look of an inquisitive rodent emerging into the daylight from the drain.
Harold Nicholson

The old woman was not only ugly with the ugliness age brings us all but showed signs of formidable ugliness by birth—pickle-jar chin, mainsail ears and a nose like a trigonometry problem. What's more, she had the deep frown and snit wrinkles that come from a lifetime of bad character.
PJ O'Rourke

Oh my God, look at you. Anyone else hurt in the accident?

Who picks your clothes—Stevie Wonder?
US comedian Don Rickles

My best birth control now is to leave the lights on.
Joan Rivers

She was so ugly she could make a mule back away from an oat bin.
Will Rogers

My teeth stuck out so far, I used to eat her kid's candy bars by accident.
Rita Rudner

Her body has gone to her head.
Barbara Stanwyck

She wears her clothes as if they were thrown on with a pitchfork.
Jonathan Swift

He was either a man of about a hundred and fifty who was rather young for his years, or a man of about a hundred and ten who had been aged by trouble.
PG Wodehouse

Insults about looks

Can I borrow your face for a few days? My arse is going on holiday.

Don't you need a license to be that ugly?

Every girl has the right to be ugly, but you abused the privilege!

Fire your wardrobe consultant.

He looked out the window and got arrested for mooning.

His mother had to be drunk to breastfeed him.

I've seen people like you before, but I had to pay admission!

I'm not as dumb as you look.

It is such a shame to ruin such beautiful blonde hair by dying your roots black.

Next time you shave, try standing an inch or two closer to the blade.

They didn't give him a costume when he auditioned for *Star Wars*.

They filmed *Gorillas in the Mist* in her shower.

They pay her to put her clothes on in strip joints.

Well, this day was a total waste of make-up for you.

Whatever kind of look you were aiming at, you missed.

When he walks past the bathroom the toilet flushes itself.

When she comes into a room, the mice jump on chairs.

When she tried entering an ugly contest they said, Sorry, no professionals.

When she walks into a bank, they turn off the surveillance cameras.

You got a face only a mother could love ... unfortunately she hates it too!

You have a very striking face! How many times have you been struck there?

You look like a professional blind date.

You look like shit. Is that the style now?

Your mouth is getting too big for your muzzle.

Fat

I'm anorexic actually. Anorexic people look in the mirror and think they look fat, and so do I.
Jo Brand

If I put on five more pounds I'll be eligible for statehood.
Audrey Buslik

My mother-in-law had to stop skipping for exercise. It registered seven on the Richter scale.
Les Dawson

I'd love to slit my mother-in-law's corsets and watch her spread to death.
Phyllis Diller

She not only kept her lovely figure, she's added so much to it.
Bob Fosse

OBESE WOMAN: I just adore nature.
GROUCHO MARX: That's loyalty, after what nature did to you.

He is so fat he hasn't seen his privates in twenty years.
Carson McCullers

The last time I saw anything like you, the whole herd had to be destroyed.
Eric Morecambe

I've lost six pounds on the way to the Super Bowl. Mind you, that's like throwing a deck chair off the Queen Mary.
Bill Parcells

Had double chins all the way down to his stomach.
Mark Twain

My doctor has advised me to give up those intimate little dinners for four, unless there are three people eating with me.
Orson Welles

Insults for the fat

At a restaurant when they give him the menu he replies, 'Yes, please'.

Doc Marten had to kill three cows just to make her a pair of shoes.

He can lie down and stand up and his height doesn't change.

He was born with a silver shovel in his mouth.

He's so fat he has the only car in town with stretch marks.

Hey! I remember you when you had only one stomach.

His cereal bowl comes with a lifeguard.

I had to take a train and two buses just to get on her good side.

She's got smaller fat women orbiting around her.

The last time I saw a figure like that it was being milked.

They say that travel broadens one. You must have been around the world.

You have an hourglass figure. Pity the sand settled in the wrong place.

When he gets in an elevator, it has to go down.

When she goes to a restaurant, she gets an estimate.

When he steps on the scale it says, 'One at a time, please.'

When she goes to an all-you-can-eat-buffet, they have to install speed bumps.

When she ran away, they had to use all four sides of the milk carton.

When she steps on the scale it says, 'Sorry, we don't do livestock'.

When she walked in front of the TV I missed three commercials.

When she was diagnosed with the flesh eating disease, the doctor gave her five years to live.

5. Men and women and other relationships

The ongoing battle between men and women only occasionally erupts into out-and-out warfare. Most of the time it's made up of a lifetime of skirmishes. As if that weren't enough the nastiness can later spread to the children.

• • • • • • •

Behind every great man, there is a surprised woman.
Maryon Elspeth Pearson, wife of Lester Bowles Pearson, the 14th Prime Minister of Canada

A wife of 40 should be like money. You should be able to change her for two of 20.

Men fantasise about being in bed with two women. Women fantasise about it too because at least they'll have someone to talk to when he falls asleep.

My husband's mind is like a Welsh railway. One track and dirty.

Women don't smoke after sex because one drag a night is enough.

Sex with a man is all right, but not as good as the real thing.
Anonymous

UK actress Dame Sybil Thorndike was married to fellow actor Sir Lewis Casson for over sixty years. She was once asked whether she had ever contemplated divorce. Her reply:
'Divorce, never. But murder, often!'

Now at least I know where he is.
Queen Alexandra on the death of her husband Edward VII

A peptic ulcer is a hole in a man's stomach through which he crawls to escape his wife.
J.A.D. Anderson

On 7 August 1821 the consort of George IV, Queen Caroline, was dying. The 26-year-long marriage had never been a happy one and both husband and wife found each other so mutually unattractive that they only had sex three times—twice on the first night of their nuptials and once on the second. As she lay on her death bed the 53-year-old insisted to her husband that he take another wife.

'Never. I will always take mistresses,' he said.
'That shouldn't hamper your marrying,' she replied.

*** *** ***

Mother nature is wonderful. She gives us twelve years to develop a love for our children before turning them into teenagers.
Eugene P. Bertin

I feel so miserable without you. It's almost like having you here.
Stephen Bishop

How I wish that Adam had died with all his ribs in his body.
Dion Boucicault

I'm not taking my wife to Paris because you don't take a sausage roll to a banquet.
Winston Churchill

An exchange between socialite Nancy Astor and Winston Churchill:
ASTOR: If you were my husband, I'd poison your coffee.
CHURCHILL: If you were my wife, I'd drink it.

I married beneath me. All women do.
Nancy Astor

*** *** ***

The fastest way to a man's heart is through his chest.
Roseanne Barr

The majority of husbands remind me of an orangutan trying to play the violin.
Honore de Balzac

Most women are not so young as they are painted.
Max Beerbohm

He was happily married—but his wife wasn't.
Victor Borge talking about Mozart

With friends like you, who needs enemas?
Matthew Broderick

It was very good of God to let Carlyle and Mrs Carlyle marry one another and so make only two people miserable instead of four.
Samuel Butler on Thomas Carlyle

The male is a domestic animal which, if treated with firmness and kindness, can be trained to do most things.
Jilly Cooper

Marriage is like putting your hand into a bag full of snakes in the hopes of pulling out an eel.
Leonardo da Vinci

She has been kissed as often as a police-court Bible, and by much the same class of people.
Robertson Davies

My wife is as cold as the hairs on a polar bear's bum.
Les Dawson

Well, at least the champagne's warm.
Benjamin Disraeli's remark at a particularly bad dinner party

My wife has a slight impediment to her speech. Every now and then she stops to breathe.
Jimmy Durante

If you can't live without me, why aren't you dead already?
Cynthia Heimel

I'm not denying that women are foolish. God Almighty made them to match men.
George Eliot

Children should neither be seen or heard from—ever again.

Women are like elephants to me: nice to look at, but I wouldn't want to own one.
WC Fields

My own, or other people's?
Peggy Guggenheim's answer to the question, 'How many husbands have you had?'

When a man steals your wife, there is no better revenge than to let him keep her.
Sacha Guitry

There are only about twenty murders a year in London and not all are serious—some are just husbands killing their wives.
GH Hatherill

I bequeath all my property to my wife on the condition that she remarry immediately. Then there will be at least one man to regret my death.
Heinrich Heine

A woman's mind is cleaner than a man's. She changes it more often.
Oliver Herford

Women's intuition is the result of millions of years of not thinking.
Rupert Hughes

Bigamy is having one husband too many. Monogamy is the same.
Erica Jong

A junior lawyer asked Lord Russell of Killowen:
'What's the heaviest penalty for bigamy?'
'Two mothers-in-law,' he answered.

A woman occasionally is quite a serviceable substitute for masturbation. It takes an abundance of imagination, to be sure.
Austrian satirist Karl Kraus

I think that husbands and wives should live in separate houses. If there's enough money, the children should live in a third.
Cloris Leachman

I've had them both, and I don't think much of either.
Actress Beatrix Lehmann commenting on a wedding in Hollywood

Teachers are overworked and underpaid. True, it is an exacting and exhausting business, this damming up the flood of human potentialities.
George B. Leonard

The people I'm furious with are the women's liberationists. They keep getting up on soapboxes and proclaiming that women are brighter than men. That's true. But it should be kept quiet or it ruins the whole racket.
Anita Loos

A woman will lie about anything, just to stay in practice.
Phillip Marlowe

I married your mother because I wanted children. Imagine my disappointment when you came along.

Women should be obscene and not heard.
Groucho Marx

Women want mediocre men, and men are working hard to become as mediocre as possible.
Anthropologist Margaret Mead

A misogynist is a man who hates women as much as women hate each other.

Love is the delusion that one woman differs from another.
HL Mencken

Men and women and other relationships

When a woman becomes a scholar there is usually something wrong with her sexual organs.
Friedrich Nietzsche

Having a family is like having a bowling alley installed in your brain.
Martin Mull

My wife is the sort of woman who gives necrophilia a bad name.

I had bad luck with both my wives. The first one left me and the second one didn't.
Patrick Murray

She should get a divorce and settle down.
Jack Paar

Like its politicians and its wars, society has the teenagers it deserves.
JB Priestly

The only original thing about some men is original sin.

When you see what some girls marry you realise how much they must hate working for a living.
Helen Rowland

When I was a little girl I had only two friends, and they were imaginary. And they would only play with each other.
Rita Rudner

I love mankind. It's people I can't stand.
Charles M. Schulz

Gee, what a terrific party. Later on we'll get some fluid and embalm each other.
Neil Simon

The male chromosome is an incomplete female chromosome. In other words the male is a walking abortion; aborted at the gene stage. To be male is to be deficient, emotionally limited; maleness is a deficiency disease and males are emotional cripples.
Valerie Solanas

Education is the inculcation of the incomprehensible into the ignorant by the incompetent.
Josiah Stamp

The great and almost only comfort about being a woman is that one can always pretend to be more stupid than one is and no-one is surprised.
Freya Stark

Every woman is entitled to a middle husband she can forget.
Adela Rogers St. Johns

A woman without a man is like a fish without a bicycle.

The surest way to be alone is to get married.
Gloria Steinem

Once a woman has given you her heart you can never get rid of the rest of her body.
John Vanbrugh

There are more men than women in mental hospitals, which just goes to show who's driving who crazy.
Peter Veale

We are so vain that we even care for the opinion of those we don't care for.
Marie von Ebner-Eschenbach

Give a man a free hand and he'll run it all over you.

His father should have thrown him away and kept the stork.
Mae West

The main difference between men and women are that men are lunatics and women are idiots.
Rebecca West

Whatever women do they must do twice as well as men to be thought half as good. Luckily this is not difficult.
Charlotte Whitton

Sex and promiscuity

There goes the famous good time that was had by all.
US actress Bette Davis

Men of every age flocked around Diana Cooper like gulls round a council tip.
John Carey

Actress Louisa Lewis was known in her day for having been very 'liberated'. When she was to be married her contemporary, actor Samuel Foote, overheard this conversation remarking on her confession of all her past dalliances to her future husband.

'What honesty she must have!' said one.
'What courage!' said another.
'What a memory!' said Foote.

🙦 🙦 🙦

Yet like a bitch she wags her tail for more.
British dramatist John Lacy on Barbara Villiers, Countess of Cleveland, Mistress to Charles II

You were born with your legs apart. They'll send you to the grave in a Y-shaped coffin.
UK playwright Joe Orton

If all the girls from [snobby private colleges] Wellesley and Vasser were laid end to end I wouldn't be a bit surprised.

That woman speaks eight languages and can't say no in any of them.
Dorothy Parker

Your idea of fidelity is not having more than one man in bed at the same time.
US Screenwriter Frederic Raphael

She's so pure, Moses couldn't even part her knees.
US comedian Joan Rivers

In order to avoid being called a flirt, she always yielded easily.
Charles, Count Talleyrand, on his contemporary Mme de Genlis

She's the kind of woman who climbed the ladder of success—wrong by wrong.

The finest woman that ever walked the streets.
Mae West

Outside every thin girl is a fat man, trying to get in.
Katharine Whitehorn

She's been on more laps than a napkin.
Walter Winchell

6. Politics

In no other arena of life do the insults fly so high or
so free. Politicians are nearly always at each others
throats, which is where many people think they should
be too. In fact, you can often follow a chain of insults in
political life unlike anywhere else. Politicians are seldom
further apart than one or two degrees of separation and
parliamentary privilege allows a freedom of expression
not granted to those of us who may have to worry
about little things like libel.

• • • • • • • •

You have all the characteristics of a popular politician: a horrible
voice, bad breeding, and a vulgar manner.
Aristophanes

Pathological exhibits ... human scum ... paranoics, degenerates,
morons, bludgers .... pack of dingoes ... industrial outlaws and
political lepers ... ratbags. If these people went to Russia, Stalin
wouldn't even use them for manure.
Australian politician Arthur Calwell on Australian communists

Ninety per cent of the politicians give the other ten per cent a bad
name.
Henry Kissinger

Democracy substitutes election by the incompetent many for
appointment by the corrupt few.
George Bernard Shaw

This party is a bit like an old stagecoach. If you drive along at a
rapid rate everyone aboard is either so exhilarated or so seasick
that you don't have a lot of difficulty.
Harold Wilson on leading the British Labour Party

Government does not solve problems. It subsidises them.

Politics is supposed to be the second oldest profession. I have come to realize that it bears a very close resemblance to the first.
Ronald Reagan

🍂 🍂 🍂

British politicians

American politicians will do anything for money; English politicians take the money and won't do anything.
Stephen Leacock

Clement Attlee, who was Deputy British Prime Minister from 1942 to 1945 and Prime Minister from 1945 to 1951, was the target of a considerable amount of invective. Consider these slurs from Winston Churchill:

He is a sheep in sheep's clothing.

A modest little man with much to be modest about.

An empty taxi arrived at 10 Downing Street, and when the door was opened, Attlee got out.

Or this one from UK writer George Orwell:

He reminds me of nothing so much as a dead fish before it has had time to stiffen.

This island is made mainly of coal and is surrounded by fish. Only an organising genius could produce a shortage of coal and fish at the same time.
Aneurin Bevan on the Tory Party

Bevan of course was himself far from being universally admired. He even felt the betrayal of his own Labour Party, at which he exclaimed:

Damn it all! You can't have the crown of thorns *and* the thirty pieces of silver!

He can hardly enter a railway train because there is no Fourth Class.
Daily Express comment on Bevan

Another frequently maligned British PM was Neville Chamberlain who is chiefly remembered for having been conned by Adolf Hitler. Churchill commented that 'an appeaser is one who feeds a crocodile hoping it will eat him last'. He also said of Chamberlain that:

At the depths of that dusty soul there is nothing but abject surrender.

He looked at foreign affairs through the wrong end of a municipal drainpipe.

A retail mind in a wholesale business.

He might make an adequate Lord Mayor of Birmingham — in a lean year.
David Lloyd George on Neville Chamberlain

Dangerous as an enemy, untrustworthy as a friend, but fatal as a colleague.
Sir Hercules Robinson on Chamberlain

Winston Churchill's long and dramatic political career lent itself to all sorts of slings and arrows. This comment he once made just about sums him up:

When I am abroad I always make it a rule never to criticise or attack the Government of my country. I make up for lost time when I am at home.

An admirer of UK politician James Keir Hardie once made this comment to Churchill:

'He is not a great politician, but he will be in heaven before you and me, Winston.'

To which Churchill replied:

'If heaven is going to be filled with people like Hardie, well the Almighty can have them all to himself.'

It is fitting that we should have buried the Unknown Prime Minister by the side of the Unknown Soldier.
Churchill's comment of the internment of Andrew Bonar Law at Westminster Abbey

There but for the grace of God, goes God.
Churchill on Stafford Cripps

There he stalks, that wuthering height.
Churchill on John Reith

In defeat unbeatable, in victory unbearable.
Churchill on General Montgomery

I thought he was a young man of promise; but it appears he was a young man of promises.
Arthur James Balfour on Winston Churchill

When I am right, I get angry. Churchill gets angry when he is wrong. We are angry at each other much of the time.
Charles de Gaulle on Winston Churchill

The greatest cross I have to bear is the cross of Lorraine.
Churchill on Charles de Gaulle

I wish Stanley Baldwin no ill, but it would have been much better if he had never lived.

He occasionally stumbled over the truth, but hastily picked himself up and hurried on as if nothing had happened.
Winston Churchill on fellow UK Prime Minister Stanley Baldwin.

Even Churchill's son, Randolph, had this to say of Baldwin:
He never believed in doing something that he could get someone else to do for him.

Not even a public figure. A man of no experience. And of the utmost inexperience.
Lord Curzon on Stanley Baldwin

I met Curzon in Downing Street, from whom I got the sort of greeting a corpse would give to an undertaker.
Stanley Baldwin on Lord Curzon

※ ※ ※

It was said Mr Gladstone could convince most people of most things, and himself of anything.
Dean William R. Inge on William Gladstone

Mr Gladstone speaks to me as if I were a public meeting.
Queen Victoria on William Gladstone

They told me how Mr Gladstone read Homer for fun, which I thought served him right.
Winston Churchill on William Gladstone

If you weren't such a great man you'd be a terrible bore.
Mrs William Gladstone to her husband.

He has committed every crime that does not require courage.
Benjamin Disraeli on Irish politician Daniel O'Connell

He traces the steam train always back to the kettle.

The right honourable gentleman is reminiscent of a poker. The only difference is that a poker gives off the occasional signs of warmth.

The right honourable gentleman's smile is like the silver fittings on a coffin.
Benjamin Disraeli on fellow British Prime Minister Robert Peel

If a traveller were informed that such a man was the leader of the House of Commons, he might begin to comprehend how the Egyptians worshipped an insect.
Benjamin Disraeli on fellow British Prime Minister Lord John Russell

He is a self-made man and worships his creator.
British statesman John Bright on Benjamin Disraeli

David Lloyd George was another British PM who both gave out and took a lot of abuse. George once called the House of Lords 'a body of 500 men chosen at random from amongst the unemployed.'

Like a cushion he always bore the impress of the last man who had sat on him.
David Lloyd George on Lord Derby

... was brilliant to the top of his army boots.
David Lloyd George on British Field Marshall Douglas Haig

The right honourable and learned gentleman has twice crossed the floor of this House, each time leaving behind a trail of slime.
David Lloyd George on Sir John Simon

He spent his whole life in plastering together the true and the false and there from manufacturing the plausible.
Stanley Baldwin on David Lloyd George

He did not seem to care which way he travelled, as long as he was in the driver's seat.
Lord Beaverbrook on David Lloyd George

Oh, if I could piss the way he speaks!
Georges Clemenceau on David Lloyd George

The happy warrior of Squandermania.
Winston Churchill on David Lloyd George

He couldn't see a belt without hitting below it.
Margot Asquith, British socialite and wife of UK Prime Minister Herbert Henry Asquith, on David Lloyd George

For twenty years he has held a season ticket on the line of least resistance, and has gone wherever the train of events has carried him, lucidly justifying his position at whatever point he has happened to find himself.
Leo Amery on Herbert Henry Asquith

Smith was famously rude to everybody. In one notable early exchange:

Court judge to Smith: 'You're very offensive, young man.'

'As a matter of fact, we both are,' Smith replied. 'The only difference between us is that I am trying to be and you can't help it.'

Perhaps it was this aspect of his personality that so appealed to his best friend Winston Churchill.
'Winston has devoted the best years of his life to preparing his impromptu speeches'
Smith once said.

Margot Asquith didn't have time for either of them:

'Very clever, but his brains go to his head,' she once said of Smith.

He would kill his own mother just so that he could use her skin to make a drum to beat his own praises.
Margot Asquith on Churchill (although this comment is also attributed to Lloyd George)

He can best be described as one of those orators who, before they get up, do not know what they are going to say; and when they are speaking do not know what they are saying; and when they have sat down, do not know what they have said.
Churchill on Lord Charles Beresford

Attlee to Churchill:

I must remind the Right Honourable Gentleman that a monologue is not a decision.

When Carter gave a fireside chat, the fire went out.
Anonymous on Jimmy Carter

Recession is when your neighbour loses his job. Depression is when you lose yours. A recovery is when Jimmy Carter loses his.
Ronald Reagan

First in ability on the list of second-rate men.
Anonymous **New York Times** writer on 21st US President Chester Alan Arthur

The worst piece of shit ever to run this country, including King George III; when's the last time a president made half his country want to move to Canada?
Beast Magazine's description of George W. Bush.

Beast has been even more disparaging of Bush's mother, Barbara:
The root of America's decay; the poison tree from whence the fruit loop George W. Bush sprang. This unfeeling, unthinking patrician hag spawned America's most notorious welfare child, whose every glaring deficiency has been excused or underwritten by undeserved wealth.

So visibly evil that all of the documented evidence against him is superfluous.

A true psychopath with only one motivating force; insatiable greed. Pathological lies change from day to day depending on which way the spin blows.

Beast Magazine's descriptions of Dick Cheney

A politician so horrible, his prior career as an exterminator constitutes fratricide.

Beast Magazine's descriptions of former US House Majority Leader Tom Delay

A greasy pig whose only distinction in life is his total lack of decency. Rove is decidedly not a genius; he is simply missing the part of his soul that prevents the rest of us from kicking elderly women in the face.

Beast Magazine's description of George W. Bush's deputy chief of staff, Karl Rove

John Major, Norman Lamont: I wouldn't spit in their mouths if their teeth were on fire.

Rodney Bickerstaff

Major is what he is: a man from nowhere, going nowhere, heading for well-merited obscurity as fast as his mediocre talents can carry him.

Paul Johnson

Thomas Dewey is just about the nastiest little man I've ever known. He struts sitting down.

Mrs Clarence Dykstra

Every drop of blood in that man's veins has eyes that look downward.

US poet Ralph Waldo Emerson on Daniel Webster

Attila the Hen.
Clement Freud on Margaret Thatcher. Neil Kinnock referred to her as the
'Plutonium Blonde'.

**The Prime Minister tells us she has given the French president a
piece of her mind, not a gift I would receive with alacrity.**
Denis Healy on Margaret Thatcher

The only thing he ever took up in university was space.
Anonymous on Denis Healey

She's a handbag communist who believes that you pay as you go.
The **New Yorker** on Margaret Thatcher

**She sounded like the _Book of Revelations_ read out over a railway
station public address system by a headmistress of a certain age
wearing calico knickers.**
Clive James on Margaret Thatcher

The Immaculate Misconception.
Norman St John-Stevas on Margaret Thatcher

🐀 🐀 🐀

Hermann Goering rudely jostles an Italian aristocrat on the platform of a railway
station. The aristocrat demands an apology:
'I am Herman Goering,' the head of the Luftwaffe says.

**The Italian replies: 'As an excuse that is inadequate, but as an
explanation it is ample.'**

**Wherever Stafford has tried to increase the sum of human
happiness, grass never grows again.**
Anonymous insult to Sir Stafford Cripps

Sir Stafford has a brilliant mind until it is made up.
Lady Violet Bonham-Carter on Sir Stafford Cripps

🐀 🐀 🐀

Richard Nixon, Gary Hart and Teddy Kennedy have just got together to form a new law firm. It's called Trickem, Dickem and Dunkem.
US writer Buffy Bluechip

I worship the quicksand he walks in.
Satirist Art Buchwald on Richard Nixon

Avoid all needle drugs. The only dope worth shooting is Richard Nixon.
US activist Abbie Hoffman

And this comment on Richard Nixon by Norman Cousins:
Nixon's motto was: If two wrongs don't make a right, try three.

And from James Reston:
He inherited some good instincts from his Quaker forebears, but by diligent hard work, he overcame them.

And from Harry S. Truman:
Richard Nixon is a no-good lying bastard. He can lie out of both sides of his mouth at the same time and if he ever caught himself telling the truth, he'd lie just to keep his hand in.

And from Adlai Stephenson:
The kind of politician who would cut down a redwood tree and then mount the stump to make a speech for conservation.

🌣🌣🌣

Garfield has shown that he is not possessed of the backbone of an angleworm.
18th US President Ulysses S. Grant on 20th US President James A. Garfield

Leon Britten looked like a bloke in the sixth form who never had a date.
Simon Hoggart

Having an argument with Geoffrey Howe is like being savaged by a dead sheep.
Denis Healey on fellow UK politician Geoffrey Howe

ELLICOTT:	I did not mislead the House.
HAYDEN:	Not intentionally. It was second nature.
SPEAKER:	Order! The honourable member for Oxley will withdraw that remark.
HAYDEN:	I apologise. I meant a second opinion.
SPEAKER:	The honourable member for Oxley will withdraw that remark.
HAYDEN:	I withdraw it. A second considered opinion.
SPEAKER:	Order! I will not persist with this. The honourable member for Oxley will withdraw unconditionally.
HAYDEN:	Whatever you say. I withdraw unconditionally.
SPEAKER:	I name the honourable member for Oxley.

Exchange between Australian politicians Bob Ellicott and Bill Hayden and the Speaker of the House.

Roosevelt proved that a man could be President for life; Truman proved that anybody could be President; and Eisenhower proved you don't need to have a President.
Georg Wilhelm Friedrich Hegel

His mind was like a soup dish, wide and shallow. It could hold a small amount of nearly anything, but the slightest jarring spilled the soup into somebody's lap.
US novelist Irving Stone on William Jennings Bryan

He has all the characteristics of a dog except loyalty.
Sam Houston on fellow US politician Thomas Jefferson Green

MacArthur is the type of man who thinks that when he gets to heaven, God will step down from the great white throne and bow him into His vacated seat.
US Secretary of the Interior Harold Ickes on Douglas MacArthur

One could drive a schooner through any part of his argument and never scrape against a fact.
David Houston on fellow US politician William Jennings Bryan

The General is suffering from mental saddle sores.
Harold Ickes on Hugh S. Johnson

The enviably attractive nephew who sings an Irish ballad for the company and then winsomely disappears before the table clearing and dishwashing begin.
Lyndon B. Johnson on JFK. Political expediency would dictate that LBJ would ultimately become JFK's Vice-President. Lee Harvey Oswald would dictate that LBJ would ultimately become JFK's successor.

You slam a politician, you make out he's the devil, with horns and hoofs. But his wife loves him, and so did all his mistresses.
UK social critic Pamela Hansford Johnson

He came out for the right side of every question always a little too late.
US writer Sinclair Lewis on abolitionist Henry Ward Beecher

He used statistics the way a drunkard uses lampposts—for support, not illumination.
Scottish writer Andrew Lang

He'll double-cross that bridge when he comes to it.
Oscar Levant on an anonymous politician

... as thin as the homeopathic soup that was made by boiling the shadow of a pigeon that had been starved to death.
Abraham Lincoln on a rival

He looks like the guy in a science fiction movie who is the first to see the Creature.
David Frye on Gerald Ford

Ronald Reagan doesn't dye his hair, he's just prematurely orange.
Gerald Ford on Ronald Reagan

I believe that Ronald Reagan can make this country what it once was—an Arctic region covered with ice.
Steve Martin

A senescent bimbo with a lust for home furnishings.
Barbara Ehrenreich on Nancy Reagan

Don't be so humble, you're not that great.
Golda Meir to Moshe Dyan

US Journalist HL Mencken was well-known in his time for his acerbic comments.
The art of running the circus from the monkey cage.
was his assessment of democracy

He sailed through American history like a steel ship loaded with monoliths of granite.
HL Mencken on Grover Cleveland

He slept more than any other president, whether by day or night. Nero fiddled, but Coolidge only snored.
HL Mencken on Calvin Coolidge

On hearing that Calvin Coolidge had died, Dorothy Parker famously said: 'How can they tell?'

Hoover, if elected, will do one thing that is almost incomprehensible to the human mind: he will make a great man out of Coolidge.
US advocate Clarence Darrow on Herbert Hoover and Calvin Coolidge

He writes the worst English that I have ever encountered. It reminds me of a string of wet sponges; it reminds me of tattered washing on the line; it reminds me of stale bean soup, of college yells, of dogs barking idiotically through endless nights. It is so bad that a sort of grandeur creeps into it. It drags itself out of the dark abysm of pish and crawls insanely up the topmost pinnacle of posh. It is rumble and bumble. It is flap and doodle. It is balder and dash.
Social critic HL Mencken on Warren G. Harding

If he became convinced tomorrow that coming out for cannibalism would get him the votes he surely needs, he would begin fattening a missionary in the White House backyard come Wednesday.
H. L. Mencken on Franklin D. Roosevelt

One could not even dignify him with the name of a stuffed shirt. He was simply a hole in the air.
George Orwell on Stanley Baldwin

Eva Peron went on a tour of Europe in 1947. Aside from a cordial fascist welcome in Spain, she was snubbed by both the British Royal family and the Pope. At one point someone in a crowd called her a whore. She complained about this to one of her hosts. The man observed: 'I haven't been on a ship in years but they still call me Admiral.'

An empty suit that goes to funerals and plays golf.
Ross Perot on Dan Quayle

CHATHAM: **If I cannot speak standing, I will speak sitting; and if I cannot speak sitting, I will speak lying.**

NORTH: **Which he will do in whatever position he speaks.**
UK politician Lord Chatham exchanging words with Lord North

I could carve out of a banana a judge with more backbone than that.
Theodore Roosevelt on US Supreme Court Justice Oliver Wendell Holmes

Two thirds mush and one-third Eleanor.
Alice Roosevelt Longworth on her distant cousin Theodore Roosevelt

He knows nothing and thinks he knows everything. That points clearly to a political career.
George Bernard Shaw

The Right Honourable Gentleman is indebted to his memory for his jests and to his imagination for his facts.
Irish playwright Richard Brinsley Sheridan on British politician Henry Dundas

He would not steal a red-hot stove.
Thaddeus Stevens on fellow US politician Simon Cameron's honesty. When called to task on the comment he said, 'I said Cameron would not steal a red-hot stove. I now withdraw that statement.'

🙵 🙵 🙵

In America any boy may become President, and I suppose that's just one of the risks he takes.

A politician is a person who approaches every subject with an open mouth.
Adlai Stevenson

If they will stop telling lies about the Democrats, we will stop telling the truth about them.

Adlai Stevenson on the Republican Party

A supporter said this to Adlai Stevenson in 1956 when he was running for President: 'Senator, you have the vote of every thinking person!'
His reply: 'That's not enough, madam, we need a majority!'

The General has dedicated himself so many times, he must feel like the cornerstone of a public building.

Adlai Stevenson on Dwight Eisenhower

We hear the Secretary of State boasting of his brinkmanship, the art of bringing us to the edge of the abyss.

Adlai Stevenson on John Foster Dulles

He thinks himself deaf because he no longer hears himself talked of.

Charles Maurice de Talleyrand-Perigord on the Vicomte de Chateaubriand

He objected to ideas only when others had them.

British historian AJP Taylor on British politician Ernest Bevin

I thought him fearfully ill-educated and quite tenth rate—pathetic. I felt quite maternal to him.

Hugh Walpole on meeting Adolf Hitler in 1925

He has a bungalow mind.

28th US President Woodrow Wilson on 29th US President Warren Harding

It is a pity, as my husband says, that more politicians are not bastards by birth instead of vocation.

Katherine Whitehorn

A triumph of the embalmer's art.

Gore Vidal on Ronald Reagan

John Wilkes was campaigning for office when he was heckled.

HECKLER: I would rather vote for the devil than for John Wilkes!

WILKES: And if your friend is not standing?

❦❦❦

Compare this exchange between another Heckler and Australian Prime Minister Robert Menzies:

HECKLER: I wouldn't vote for you if you were the Archangel Gabriel!

MENZIES: If I were the Archangel Gabriel you would scarcely be in my constituency!

❦❦❦

He immatures with age.
Harold Wilson on Tony Benn

7. Royalty

There's an old saying that the higher a monkey climbs, the more you can see his backside. Royalty, born at the top of the tree, show more of their backside than most and are ripe for the picking, if you get my meaning.

• • • • • • •

The British people prefer their royalty stupid, selfish and greedy. The more ridiculous and philistine they are, the easier it is to identify with them.
Sunday reporter Paul Foot

John Wilkes once toasted the health of George III in the presence of his heir apparent, the Prince of Wales, the future George IV. This was an unprecedented event since George III was greatly disliked.Knowing this the Prince asked Wilkes how long he had shown such concern over his father's health.

'Since I had the pleasure of your Royal Highness' acquaintance,' Wilkes replied.

George VI asked a new acquaintance, 'Young man, do you play cards?'
'No, your Majesty,' he replied, 'seeing I cannot tell the difference between a king and a knave.'

Elizabeth II was riding in a carriage with an African dignitary when one of the horses broke wind.

QUEEN: Oh, I'm awfully sorry.

DIGNITARY: Oh, that's quite all right, Your Majesty. If you hadn't spoken I'd have thought it was the horse.

8. Acute and funny

Some comments simply defy easy classification.

• • • • • • • •

A gentleman is one who never hurts anyone's feelings unintentionally.
Oscar Wilde

Lack of education is an extraordinary handicap when one is being offensive.
Josephine Tey

Only a dog owner is insane enough to watch a dog lick its balls, eat its own barf, drink out of the toilet, and then think the animal loves them when it licks their face.
Anonymous

Adam was the luckiest man in the world. He had no mother-in-law.
Sholom Aleichem

Margot Asquith, obliged to entertain people she didn't like, would invite them all at once to her house and then retire to her room to play bridge with her friends.

Once one of her guests met her later and said, 'Oh, Lady Asquith, I hope you are well. I was at your party last night.'

To which Asquith replied, 'Thank God I wasn't.'

What an inspiration she must be to android researchers everywhere.
Beast Magazine's description of George W. Bush's First Lady, Laura

We are all born mad. Some remain so.
Samuel Beckett

My piles bleed for you.
Herbert Beerbohm Tree

Exchange between John Wilmot, Second Earl of Rochester, and UK theologian Isaac Barrow:

ROCHESTER: Doctor, I am yours to my shoe tie.

BARROW: My Lord, I am yours to the ground.

ROCHESTER: Doctor, I am yours to the centre.

BARROW: My Lord, I am yours to the antipodes.

ROCHESTER: Doctor, I am yours to the lowest pit of hell.

BARROW: And there, my Lord, I leave you.

Reinhart was never his mother's favorite—and he was an only child.
Thomas Berger

A Boy Scout Troup is a lot of boys dressed as jerks, led by a jerk dressed as a boy.
Shelley Berman

Santa Claus has the right idea. Visit people only once a year.
Victor Borge

We invite people like that to tea, but we don't marry them.
Lady Chetwode on her future son-in-law, John Betjeman

Cultured people are merely the glittering scum which floats upon the deep river of production.
Winston Churchill

UK LABOUR POLITICIAN BESSIE BRADDOCK TO WINSTON CHURCHILL AT A PARTY:
Winston, you're drunk.

CHURCHILL: Bessie, you're ugly. And tomorrow morning I'll be sober.

WC Fields once also made a similar comment:

I'll be sober tomorrow, but you'll be crazy for the rest of your life.

I've had a perfectly wonderful evening. But this wasn't it.
Groucho Marx

Another train incident, this time with Sir Thomas Beecham. A lady enters his 'No-Smoking Carriage', lights up and then says 'I'm sure you won't mind if I smoke.'

BEECHAM: Not at all—providing that you don't mind if I'm sick.

PASSENGER: You don't seem to realise who I am! I am one of the director's wives!

BEECHAM: If you were the director's only wife, I should still be sick.

However the more modern reply to anyone who asks 'you don't mind if I smoke?' is more generally a variation on 'not at all—providing that you don't mind if I belch/fart.'

Sir Thomas Beecham was asked if he'd ever stayed at a particular country estate.

'Yes, I spent a month down there last week-end', he replied.

I've just learned about his illness. Let's hope it's nothing trivial.
Irvin S. Cobb

I am free of all prejudices. I hate everyone equally.
WC Fields

A woman at a dinner party asked UK actress Beatrice Lillie if the pearls on her necklace were real. When Lillie replied, 'Yes,' the woman reached across the table, grabbed the pearls and tried to run them across her teeth. The woman then declared: 'They're not! They're cultured.' Lillie replied, 'How would you know, with false teeth?'

He is alive, but only in the sense that he cannot be legally buried.
Geoffrey Madan

What smells so? Has somebody been burning a rag or is there a dead mule in the backyard? No, the man is smoking a five-cent cigar.
Eugene Field

OLD VICAR:	I want to thank you, Mr Marx, for all the enjoyment you've given the world.
MARX:	And I want to thank you for all the enjoyment you've taken out of it.

A friend of Dorothy Parker commented on the other people in a party:
'Where on earth do all these people come from?'
Parker replied, 'I think after it's all over, they crawl back into the woodwork.'

Clare Boothe Luce as she meets Dorothy Parker in front of a door:
'Age before beauty,'
Parker, entering first: 'And pearls before swine.'

She was one of those women who go through life demanding to see the manager.
G. Patrick

I once had a rose named after me and was very flattered. But I was not pleased to read the description in the catalogue: no good in bed, but fine up against a wall.
Eleanor Roosevelt

❦ ❦ ❦

One can always be kind to people about whom one cares nothing.
Oscar Wilde. But Wilde didn't always get the last laugh:

WILDE:	Do you mind if I smoke?
SARAH BERNHARDT:	I don't care if you burn.

❦ ❦ ❦

VISTORS:	Good morning, we are Jehovah's Witnesses.
SHAW:	Good morning. I'm Jehovah. How are we doing?

George Bernard Shaw deals with religious house-callers

❦ ❦ ❦

If God has made us in his image we have certainly returned the compliment.
Voltaire

9. Random acts of rudeness

All that you are you owe to your parents. Why don't you send them a penny and square the account?

Anyone who told you to be yourself couldn't have given you worse advice.

As an outsider, what do you think of the human race?

Better at sex than anyone; now all he needs is a partner.

Do you ever wonder what life would be like if you'd had enough oxygen at birth?

Do you want people to accept you as you are or do you want them to like you?

Go ahead, tell them everything you know. It'll only take 10 seconds.

Have you considered suing your brains for non-support?

He is the kind of a man that you would use as a blueprint to build an idiot.

He's not stupid; he's possessed by a retarded ghost.

How did you get here? Did someone leave your cage open?

I hear the only place you're ever invited is outside.

I hear you were born on a farm. Any more in the litter?

I heard you went to have your head examined but the doctors found nothing there.

I'd like to help you out. Which way did you come in?

I hear that when your mother first saw you, she decided to leave you on the front steps of a police station while she turned herself in.

I'd like to leave you with one thought ... but I'm not sure you have anywhere to put it!

I'd like to see things from your point of view but I can't seem to get my head that far up my arse.

I'll never forget the first time we met—although I'll keep trying.

I'm busy now. Can I ignore you some other time?

Learn from your parents' mistakes—use birth control!

Pardon me, but you've obviously mistaken me for someone who gives a damn.

People can't say that you have absolutely nothing! After all, you have inferiority!

People say that you are the perfect idiot. I say that you are not perfect, but you are doing all right.

10. Insults international

Why should we restrict ourselves to individuals when cities, states, nations and even whole civilisations are up for grabs? Countries insulting each other has a long history.

• • • • • • • •

Trust a Brahman before a snake, and a snake before a harlot, and a harlot before an Afghan.
Hindu saying

Mohandas (aka Mahatma) Ghandi on Western civilisation: I think it would be a very good idea.

There have been many definitions of hell, but for the English the best definition is that it is the place where the Germans are the police, the Swedish are the comedians, the Italians are the defence force, Frenchmen dig the roads, the Belgians are the pop singers, the Spanish run the railways, the Turks cook the food, the Irish are the waiters, the Greeks run the government, and the common language is Dutch.
David Frost and Anthony Jay

Africa

If there is any place where love is dead, it is here.
Mary Benson

'Diarrhoea City'! Oh fuck yes, terrible place. You don't even have to eat anything for that. It's the dust from the camel shit. One of the worst places I've ever been.
Michael Caine on Morocco

The desert of Danakil is part of the world that the Creator must have fashioned when He was in a bad mood.
Ladislas Farago

It looks as if it has been dropped, piecemeal, from an aeroplane carrying rubbish ...
John Gunther on Africa

The less said about Massawa the better. It was one of those dark patches that are best forgotten.
Geoffrey Harmsworth

The name, which means 'my joy' in Amharic, seems peculiarly inappropriate.
Paul Henze on Dese in Ethiopia

The USA

New Jersey, the only place in the world where the air has an octane rating.

San Fran is like granola ... full of fruits and nuts.

The only difference between winter in Seattle and summer in Seattle is that in summer the rain is warmer.

You have an Austrian, anti-immigration governor. God help you Americans, you're going to need it.
Anonymous

California is a fine place to live. If you happen to be an orange
Fred Allen

You wonder about a country where the bombs are smarter than the high school graduates. At least the bombs can find Iraq on the map.
Whitney Brown

In California everyone goes to a therapist, is a therapist or is a therapist going to a therapist.
Truman Capote

We were taken to a fast food café where our order was fed into a computer. Our hamburgers, made from the flesh of chemically impregnated cattle, had been broiled over counterfeit charcoal,

placed between slices of artificially flavoured cardboard and served to us by recycled juvenile delinquents.
Jean-Michel Chapereau

Americans always try to do the right thing—after they've tried everything else.
Winston Churchill

America is the only nation in history which miraculously has gone from barbarism to degeneration without the usual interval of civilisation.
French Statesman Georges Clemenceau

American women mostly have their clothes arranged for them. And their faces too, I think.
Noel Coward

In America sex is an obsession, in other parts of the world it is a fact.
Marlene Dietrich

No one can be as calculatedly rude as the British, which amazes Americans, who do not understand studied insult and can only offer abuse as a substitute.
US writer Paul Gallico

The organisation of American society is an interlocking system of semi-monopolies notoriously venal, an electorate notoriously unenlightened, misled by a mass media notoriously phoney.
US writer Paul Goodman

McDonald's in Tokyo is a terrible revenge for Pearl Harbour.
SL Hayakawa

I don't see much future for the Americans. Everything about the behaviour of the American society reveals that it's half judaized, and the other half is negrified. How can one expect a state like that to hold together?
Adolf Hitler

America is a melting pot, the people at the bottom get burned while all the scum floats to the top.
Charlie King

Never criticise Americans. They have the best taste that money can buy.
Miles Kington

This is the most exciting place in the world to live. There are so many ways to die here.
Denis Leary on New York City

If you're going to America, bring your own food.
Fran Lebowitz

Americans are people who laugh at African witch doctors and spend 100 million dollars on fake reducing systems.
US Writer LL Levinson

The trouble with America is that there are far too many wide-open spaces surrounded by teeth.
American writer Charles Luckman

There's nothing wrong with Southern California that a rise in the ocean level wouldn't cure.
Ross MacDonald

QUESTIONER TO US CRITIC H.L. MENCKEN:

> If you find so much that is unworthy of reverence in the United States, why do you live here?

MENCKEN: Why do men go to zoos?

No-one ever went broke underestimating the taste of the American public.
HL Mencken

Hollywood is a sewer with service from the Ritz.
William Mizner

The American political system is like fast food: mushy, insipid, made out of disgusting parts of things and everybody wants some.

The Americans don't really understand what's going on in Bosnia. To them it's the unspellables killing the unpronounceables.
US Satirist PJ O'Rourke echoing Oscar Wilde's famous definition of the British upper classes at a fox hunt: the unspeakable in full pursuit of the uneatable.

If you stay in Beverly Hills too long you become a Mercedes.
Robert Redford

The national dish of America is menus.
UK broadcaster Robert Robinson

Why don't they pass a constitutional amendment prohibiting anyone from learning anything? If it works as good as Prohibition did, in five years Americans would be the smartest race of people on earth.
Will Rogers

Frustrate a Frenchman, he will drink himself to death; an Irishman, he will die of angry hypertension; a Dane, he will shoot himself; an American, he will get drunk, shoot you, then establish a million dollar aid programme for your relatives. Then he will die of an ulcer.
Canadian psychologist SA Rudin

America ... where laws and customs alike are based on the dreams of spinsters.
British philosopher Bertrand Russell

Here is the difference between Dante, Milton and me. They wrote about hell and never saw the place. I wrote about Chicago after looking the town over for years and years.
US poet Carl Sandburg

If I owned Texas and Hell, I would rent out Texas and live in Hell.
General PH Sherican

The American male doesn't mature until he has exhausted all other possibilities.
US writer Wilfred Sheed

One of the most popular Soviet meals is the bread sandwich. That is two slices of bread with another slice of bread in between. They have the same thing in America. It's called a Big Mac.
Yakov Smirnoff

Insults international

In America any boy may become President, and I suppose that's just the risk he takes.
Adlai Stevenson

I found there a country with thirty-two religions and only one sauce.
French diplomat Charles-Maurice de Talleyrand Perigord

The difference between Los Angeles and yoghurt is that yoghurt has real culture.
Tom Taussik

America ... just a nation of two hundred million used car salesmen with all the money we need to buy guns and no qualms about killing anybody else in the world who tries to make us uncomfortable.
US journalist Hunter S. Thompson

America is a large, friendly dog in a very small room. Every time it wags its tail it knocks over a chair.
UK Historian Arnold Toynbee

Speaking of New York as a traveller I have to faults to find with it. In the first place there is nothing to see; and in the second place there is no mode of getting about to see anything.
UK novelist Anthony Trollope

The hatred Americans have for their own government is pathological ... at one level it is simply thwarted greed: since our religion is making a buck, giving a part of that buck to any government is an act against nature.
Gore Vidal

In America the President rules for four years and journalism governs for ever and ever.

Of course, America had often been discovered before Columbus, but it had always been hushed up.

When good Americans die, they go to Paris; when bad Americans die, they go to America.
Oscar Wilde

Australia

In America, only the successful writer is important, in France all writers are important, in England no writer is important, and in Australia you have to explain what a writer is.
Geoffrey Cottrell. Compare also Phyllis McGinley's comment: 'In Australia, not reading poetry is a national pastime.'

The broad Australian accent is not a lovesome thing, I grant you. At its worst, it is reminiscent of a dehydrated crow uttering its last statement on life from the bough of a dead tree in the middle of a clay-pan at the peak of a seven-year drought.
Buzz Kennedy

Australia may be the only country in the world in which the term 'academic' is regularly used as a term of abuse.
Dame Leonie Kramer

To live in Australia permanently is rather like going to a party and dancing all night with your mother.
Barry Humphries

QANTAS is a condom on the penis of progress.
Ian Tuxworth on the Australian national airline

Canada

Canada has a climate nine months winter and three months late in the fall.
American saying

Montreal is the only place where a good French accent isn't a social asset.
Brendan Behan

Canada is a country so square that even the female impersonators are women.
Richard Brenner

I don't even know what street Canada is on.
Al Capone

The left in Canada is more gauche than sinister.
John Harney

In any world menu, Canada must be considered the vichyssoise of nations. It's cold, half-French and difficult to stir.
Stuart Keate

The purity of the air of Newfoundland is without doubt due to the fact that the people never open their windows.
JG Millais

A sub-artic lumber village converted by Royal Mandate into a political cock fighting pit.
Goldwin Smith on Ottawa

I fear that I have not got much to say about Canada, not having seen much; what I got by going to Canada was a cold.
Henry David Thoreau

You know that these two nations are at war for a few acres of snow, and they are spending ... more than all of Canada is worth.
Voltaire on the fight between the British and French over Canada

It makes little difference, Canada is useful only to provide me with furs.
Madame de Pompadour on the same subject after the fall of Quebec in 1759

China

Cantonese will eat anything in the sky but airplanes, anything in the sea but submarines and anything with four legs but the table.
Amanda Bennett

There are only two kinds of Chinese—those who give bribes and those who take them.
Russian saying

Cyprus

In Cyprus, three things are cheap wholesale but expensive retail: salt, sugar and whores.
Greek saying

Realising they will never be a world power, the Cypriots have decided to settle for being a world nuisance.
George Mikes

The Netherlands

Apart from cheese and tulips, the main product of Holland is advocaat, a drink made from lawyers.

The Dutch fall into two quite distinct physical types—the small, corpulent, red-faced Edams and then thinner, paler, larger Goudas.
British Humorist Alan Coren

The indigested vomit of the sea
Fell to the Dutch by just propriety.
English poet Andrew Marvell

The UK

Englishwomen's shoes look as if they had been made by someone who had often heard shoes described, but had never seen any.
Anonymous

On a fine day the climate of England is like looking up a chimney, on a foul day it is like looking down.
Anonymous

Q: Why does the River Mersey run through Liverpool?
A: If it walked it would get mugged.
Anonymous

The English instinctively admire any man who has no talent and is modest about it.
British theatre critic James Agate

English coffee tastes like water that has been squeezed out of a wet sleeve.
Fred Allen

England will fight to the last American.
Slogan of the America First Committee protesting the US involvement in World War I

Coffee in England always tastes like a chemistry experiment.
Agatha Christie

It is impossible to obtain a conviction for sodomy from a British jury. Half of them don't believe that it can physically be done, the other half are doing it.
Winston Churchill

The English think that incompetence is the same thing as sincerity.
Quentin Crisp

Freedom of discussion is in England little else than the right to write or say anything which a jury of twelve shopkeepers think it expedient should be said or written.
British historian AV Dicey

Paralytic sycophants, effete betrayers of humanity, carrion-eating servile imitators, arch-cowards and collaborators, gang of women-murderers, degenerate rabble, parasitic traditionalists, playboy soldiers, conceited dandies.
The list of 'approved terms of abuse' from the East German Communist Party for East Germans when describing Britain

It is an Englishman's privilege to grumble.
English saying

The Englishman who has lost his fortune is said to have died of a broken heart.
Ralph Waldo Emerson

All Englishmen talk as if they've got a bushel of plums stuck in their throats, and then after swallowing them get constipated from the pips.

English vegetables taste as though they have been boiled in a strong soap.
WC Fields

A broad definition of crime in England is that it is any lower-class activity that is displeasing to the upper class.
David Frost and Anthony Jay

Among three Italians will be found two clergymen; three Spaniards two braggarts; among three Germans two soldiers; among three Frenchmen, two chefs, and among three Englishmen two whoremongers.

The German originates it, the French imitate it and the Englishman exploits it.
German sayings

Britain is the only country in the world where 'too clever by half' is an insult.
AA Gill

England has become a squalid, uncomfortable, ugly place ... an intolerant, racist, homophobic, narrow-minded, authoritarian, rat-hole run by vicious, suburban-minded, materialistic philistines.
British writer Hanif Kureishi

The main difference between an Essex girl and a shopping trolley is that a shopping trolley has a mind of its own.
Ray Leigh

We know of no spectacle so ridiculous as the British public in one of its periodical fits of morality.
British historian Thomas Babington Macaulay

[England is] like a prostitute who, having sold her body all her life, decides to quit and close her business, and then tells everybody she wants to be chaste and protect her flesh as if it were jade.
Chinese politician He Manzi

England is, after all, the land where children are beaten, wives and babies bashed, football hooligans crunch, and Miss Whip and Miss Lash ply their trade as nowhere else in the Western world. Despite our belief [that] we are a 'gentle' people we have, in reality, a cruel and callous streak in our sweet natures, reinforced by a decadent puritan strain which makes some of us believe that suffering, whether useful or not, is a fit scourge to the wanton soul.
British writer Colin MacInnes

Britain is the only country in the world where the food is more dangerous than the sex.
Jackie Mason

Continental people have a sex life; the English have hot-water bottles.
Hungarian writer George Mikes

The people of England are never so happy as when you tell them they are ruined.
British writer Arthur Murray

England is a nation of shopkeepers.

The English have no exalted sentiments. They can all be bought.
Napoleon

The British have three qualities: humour, tenacity and realism. I sometimes think that we are still at the humour stage.
French President Georges Pompidou

An Englishman does everything on principle: he fights you on patriotic principles; he robs you on business principles; he enslaves you on imperial principles.

Englishmen never will be slaves; they are free to do whatever the government and public opinion allow them.

The ordinary Britisher imagines that God is an Englishman.
George Bernard Shaw

Silence: A conversation with an Englishman.
Goldwin Smith

I know why the sun never sets on the British Empire: God wouldn't trust an Englishman in the dark.
Duncan Spaeth

The English think soap is civilisation.
German philosopher Heinrich von Treitschke

An Englishman will burn his bed to catch a flea.
Turkish saying

The way to endure summer in England is to have it framed and glazed in a comfortable room.
Horace Walpole

In England we have come to rely upon a comfortable time-lag of a century intervening between the perception that something ought to be done and a serious attempt to do it.
H. G. Wells

In England it is enough for a man to try and produce any serious, beautiful work to lose all his rights as a citizen.

The English public takes no interest in a work of art until it is told that the work in question is immoral.

Thinking is the most unhealthy thing in the world, and people die of it just as they die of any other disease. Fortunately, in England at any rate, thought is not catching.

To disagree with three-fourths of the British public on all points is one of the first elements of sanity, one of the deepest consolations in all moments of spiritual doubt.
Oscar Wilde, who experienced first hand the observation of Ted Whitehead: 'Under the English legal system, you are innocent until you are shown to be Irish.'

The English have an extraordinary ability for flying into a great calm.
US writer Alexander Woollcott

France

'Escargot' is French for 'fat crawling bag of phlegm.'
Dave Barry

France was long a despotism tempered by epigrams.
Thomas Carlyle

It took no more effort than casting a Frenchman into Hell.
Dutch sayings

The friendship of the French is like their wine, exquisite, but of short duration.
German sayings

Paris is like a whore, from a distance she seems ravishing, you can't wait until you have her in your arms. Five minutes later you feel empty, disgusted with yourself. You feel tricked.
Henry Miller

The ignorance of French society gives one a rough sense of the infinite.
French philologist Joseph E. Renan

The French are sawed-off sissies who eat snails and slugs and cheese that smells like people's feet. Utter cowards who force their own children to drink wine, they gibber like baboons even when you try to speak to them in their own wimpy language.
PJ O'Rourke

FRENCH NOVELIST PAUL BOURGET TO MARK TWAIN:
Life can never be entirely dull to an American. When he has nothing else to do he can always spend a few years trying to discover who his grandfather was.

TWAIN: Right, your Excellency. But I reckon a Frenchman's got a little standby for a dull time too. He can turn in and see if he can find out who his father was.

Germany

When the Russian steals, he does it that he might have enough for himself for a single day, but when the German steals he takes enough for his children and the morrow.
German saying

The German mind has a talent for making no mistakes but the very greatest.
Clifton Fadiman

Wherever Germans are, it is unhealthy for Italians.
Italian saying

You can always reason with a German. You can always reason with a barnyard animal, too, for all the good it does.

PJ O'Rourke, echoing a Lithuanian saying:
He's like a German. He can't understand a reasonable man.

One German a beer, two Germans an organisation, three Germans a war.
Polish saying

Life is too short to learn German.
Richard Porson

Holy Roman Emperor Charles V also expressed a similar sentiment:
'I speak Spanish to God, Italian to women, French to men, and German to my horse.'

And this from the American satirists, National Lampoon:
German is a language which was developed solely to afford the speaker the opportunity to spit at strangers under the guise of polite conversation.

The East German manages to combine a Teutonic capacity for bureaucracy with a Russian capacity for infinite delay.
Goronwy Rees

One thing I will say for the Germans, they are always perfectly willing to give somebody else's land to somebody else.
Will Rogers

Greece

After shaking hands with a Greek, count your fingers.
Albanian saying

Few things can be less tempting or dangerous than a Greek woman of the age of thirty.
John Carne

The Greeks—dirty and impoverished descendants of a bunch of la-de-da fruit salads who invented democracy and then forgot how to use it while walking around dressed up like girls.
PJ O'Rourke

India

The Indian wears seven veils, which must be removed if his true face is to be seen.
English saying

Delhi is the capital of the losing streak. It is the metropolis of the crossed wire, the missed appointment, the puncture, the wrong number.
Jan Morris

Ireland

Other people have a nationality. The Irish and the Jews have a psychosis.
Brendan Behan

This is one race of people for whom psychoanalysis is of no use whatsoever.
Sigmund Freud

The Irish are a fair people, they never speak well of one another.
Samuel Johnson

Italy at least, has two things to balance its miserable poverty and mismanagement: a lively intellectual movement and a good climate. Ireland is Italy without these two.
James Joyce

The problem with Ireland is that it's a country full of genius, but with absolutely no talent.
Hugh Leonard

An Irish homosexual is one who prefers women to drink.
Sean O'Faolain

I showed my appreciation of my native land in the usual Irish way by getting out of it as soon as I possibly could.

Put an Irishman on a spit and you can always find another one to turn him.
George Bernard Shaw

Italy

The Germans really seem to have it in for the Italians. Consider this collection of sayings:

An arse in Germany is a professor in Rome.

Half an Italian in a house is one too many.

If lies were Italian, he'd make a good interpreter.

If there is a Hell, Rome is built on top of it.

Italy is a paradise for horses and hell for women.

Italy is a paradise inhabited by devils.

Italy is the paradise of the flesh, the hell of the soul, the purgatory of the pocketbook.

Italy might well be called a paradise; for whoever gets there readily falls into sin.

To cook an egg, to make a bed for a dog, and to teach an Italian to do anything are three hard things.

The Italian takes the money from the Church, and the Church from all the world.
Sir John Gielgud

Rome reminds me of a man who lives by exhibiting to travellers his grandmother's corpse.
James Joyce

Japan

The Japanese have almost as big a reputation for cruelty as do young children.
Dennis Bloodworth

The Japanese have perfected good manners and made them indistinguishable from rudeness.
Paul Theroux

Mexico

Mexican food is delicious and perfectly safe as long as you are careful never to get any of it into your digestive system.
Dave Barry

Poor Mexico, so far from God and so close to the United States.
Porfirio Diaz

You don't eat Mexican food. You just rent it.
Alexei Sayle

New Zealand

I find it hard to say if I liked the place—when I was there it appeared to be shut.
Clement Freud

Poland

Poland is now a totally independent nation, and it has managed to greatly improve its lifestyle thanks to the introduction of modern Western conveniences such as food.
Dave Barry

Russia and the Soviet Union

In Russia a man is called reactionary if he objects to having his property stolen and his wife and children murdered.
Winston Churchill

A more lifeless, depressing city does not exist on the face of the planet. Even Siberians call this 'The End of the World'.
Harry de Windt on Moscow

Moscow, as I saw it once, is Horrorsville.
James Kirkup

Los Angeles without the sun or grass.
Lillian Hellman on Moscow

Russians will consume marinated mushrooms and vodka, salted herring and vodka, smoked salmon and vodka, salami and vodka, caviar on brown bread and vodka, pickled cucumbers and vodka, cold tongue and vodka, red beet salad and vodka, scallions and vodka—anything and everything and vodka.
Hedrick Smith

Scotland

The Scotchman is one who keeps the Sabbath and every other thing he can lay his hands on.
American saying

The great thing about Glasgow now is that if there is a nuclear attack it'll look exactly the same afterwards.
Billy Connolly

Much may be made of a Scotsman, if he is caught young.

Scotland is a vile country, though God made it, but we must remember that he made it for Scotsmen, and comparisons are odious, but God also made Hell.
Samuel Johnson

The kilt is an unrivalled garment for fornication and diarrhoea.
John Masters

It requires a surgical operation to get a joke well into a Scotsman's understanding.
Sydney Smith

Switzerland

A country to be in for two hours, to two and a half if the weather is fine, and no more. Ennui comes in the third hour, and suicide attacks you before the night.
Lord Brougham

Since its national products—snow and chocolate—both melt, the cuckoo clock was invented solely in order to give tourists something solid to remember it by.
Alen Coren

Switzerland has produced the numbered bank account, Ovaltine and Valium.
Peter Freedman

Turkey

If you can imagine a man having a vasectomy without anaesthetic to the sound of frantic sitar playing, you will have some idea of what popular Turkish music is like.
Bill Bryson

That was too cruel even for a Turk.
Dutch saying

A practical joke played on history.
Peter Forster

Wales

Show a Welshman 1001 exits and he will go through the one marked 'self-destruction'.

Richard Burton

11. All the way to the grave

Who said that the last word can't be an insult? Why confine bile and venom to people who are alive? Why should the living have all the fun—especially since the dead can't answer back?

• • • • • • •

I have never killed a man, but I have read many obituaries with great pleasure.
Clarence Darrow

He'd make a lovely corpse.
Charles Dickens

Here Lies
Ezekail Aikle
Aged 102
The Good
Die Young
Anonymous

Here lies the mother of children seven
Four on earth and three in heaven
The three in heaven preferring rather
To die with mother than live with father
On a Birmingham tombstone

Here lies my wife: here let her lie!
Now she's at rest and so am I
John Dryden's suggestion for his wife's tombstone

He makes a very handsome corpse and becomes his coffin prodigiously.
Oliver Goldsmith

Posterity will ne'er survey a nobler grave than this;
Here lie the bones of Castlereagh:
Stop, traveller, and piss.
Lord Byron with a suggestion for the epitaph of British Foreign Minister Viscount Castlereagh, whom Byron also referred to once as an 'intellectual eunuch'.

I didn't attend the funeral, but I sent a nice letter saying I approved of it.
Mark Twain

And here is the longest insult in this book. British satirist Dr John Arbuthnot on the British brothel keeper, gambler and money-lender, Francis Chartres:

HERE continueth to rot The Body of FRANCIS CHARTRES, Who with inflexible constancy, And Inimitable Uniformity of Life Persisted In spite of Age and Infirmities In the Practice of Every Human Vice; Excepting Prodigality and Hypocrisy: His insatiable Avarice exempted him from the first, His matchless Impudence from the second. Nor was he more singular in the undeviating Pravity of his Manners than successful In Accumulating WEALTH. For without Trade or Profession, Without Trust of Public Money, And without Bribe-worthy service He acquired, or more properly created A Ministerial Estate. He was the only Person of his Time Who cou'd cheat without the Mask of Honesty Retain his Primeval Meanness When possess'd of Ten Thousand a Year. And having daily deserved the Gibbet for what he did, Was at last condemn'd to it for what he could not do. Oh Indignant Reader! Think not his Life useless to Mankind! Providence conniv'd at his execrable Designs, To give to After-ages A conspicuous Proof and Example, Of how small Estimation is Exorbitant Wealth in the sight of GOD, By his bestowing it on the most Unworthy of ALL MORTALS.

12. The world of work

Here are some jibes you can take to your place of
employment for those days when you remember that
'work' is a four-letter-word and that morons surround you.
Note also that some professions attract more insults than
others. Particularly lawyers. I can't imagine why.

• • • • • • •

And when you're done insulting people, you can insult consumerism
and technology.

Auditors are the troops who watch a battle from the safety of a
hillside and, when the battle is over, come down to count the dead
and bayonet the wounded.
Anonymous

There are worse things in life than death. Have you ever spent an
evening with an insurance salesman?
Woody Allen

The Metropolitan Police Force is abbreviated to the MET to give
more members a chance of spelling it.
Mike Barfield

A group of white South Africans recently killed a black lawyer
because he was black. That was wrong. The should have killed him
because he was a lawyer.
Whitney Brown

I was under the care of a couple of medical students who couldn't
diagnose a decapitation.
Jeffrey Bernard

The only difference between doctors and lawyers is that lawyers
merely rob you, whereas doctors rob you and kill you too.
Anton Chekhov

When I take up assassination, I shall start with the surgeons and work my way up to the gutter.
Dylan Thomas

Doctors prescribe medicines of which they know little, to cure diseases of which they know less, in human beings of which they know nothing.
Voltaire

Chess is the most elaborate waste of human intelligence outside an advertising agency.
Raymond Chandler

Don't tell my mother I work in an advertising agency. She thinks I play piano in a whorehouse.
Jacques Seguela

I find it rather easy to portray a businessman. Being bland, rather cruel and incompetent comes naturally to me.

Our experts describe you as an appallingly dull fellow, unimaginative, timid, spineless, easily dominated, no sense of humor, tedious company and irrepressibly drab and awful. And whereas in most professions these would be considered drawback, in accountancy they are a positive boon.
John Cleese

An actuary is someone who can't stand the excitement of chartered accountancy.
Glan Thomas

Actuaries have a reputation of being about as interesting as the footnotes on a pension plan.
George Pitcher

My definition of utter waste is a coach load of lawyers going over a cliff with three empty seats.
Lamar Hunt

The world of work

There are three reasons why lawyers are replacing rats as laboratory research animals. One is that they are plentiful, another is that lab assistants don't get so attached to them and the third thing is that you can get them to do things that you just can't get rats to do.
Blanche Knott

The OJ Simpson jury they ended up choosing had to swear they'd never heard about a case that had been in the papers every day for a year and a half. And then they asked them to rule on DNA. These idiots didn't even get that far in the alphabet. They wondered why the N came before the A.
Jackie Mason

A jury is a group of twelve people who, having lied to the judge about their hearing, health and business engagements, have failed to fool him.
HL Mencken

A lawyer will do anything to win a case. Sometimes he will even tell the truth.
Patrick Murray

An incompetent lawyer can delay a trial for months or years. A competent lawyer can delay one even longer.
Evelle J. Younger

She's a good lawyer, but 'finesse' and Marcia Clark should not be used in the same sentence.
Henry Weinstein on the chief prosecutor on the OJ Simpson trial

☛ ☛ ☛

As repressed sadists are supposed to become policemen or butchers, so those with an irrational fear of life become publishers.
Cyril Connolly

Of course prostitutes have babies. Where do you think traffic wardens come from?
Dave Dutton

If you think your boss is stupid remember; you wouldn't have your job if he were any smarter.
Albert Grant

Most of my contemporaries at school entered the World of Business, the logical destiny of bores.
Barry Humphries

An organisation is like a septic tank. The really big chunks always rise to the top.
John Imhoff

What I can't understand about Castlemaine XXXX is how they got the cat to squat over the can.
Glenn Lazarus

A committee is a cul-de-sac into which ideas are lured and then quietly strangled.
John A. Lincoln

A good rule of thumb is if you've made it to thirty-five and your job still requires you to wear a nametag, you've probably made a serious vocational error.
Dennis Miller

The only difference between a dead skunk lying on the road and a dead lawyer lying on the road is that there are skid marks near the skunk.
Patrick Murray

If brains were a virus, policemen would be the healthiest people in the world.
John O'Dwyer

The schoolteacher is certainly underpaid as a child-minder, but ludicrously over-paid as an educator.
John Osborne

My boss has the brains of Einstein's—dead since 1955.
Gene Perret

The upper crust is just a bunch of crumbs held together by dough.
Joseph A. Thomas

Fire the whole purchasing department. They'd hire Einstein and then turn down his requisition for a blackboard.
Robert Townsend

An expert is one who knows so much about so little that he neither can be contradicted, nor is worth contradicting.
Henry Ward

Insults at work

Bosses are like nappies: always on your arse and full of shit.

I need a job that has more prestige and paid better, so I'll be working at a hospital, waiting for little kids to crap out the coins they swallowed.

I really wish they wouldn't provide lunch during meetings. It just gives my manager more time to bullshit about things he has no clue over.

I'd imagine you as a leader of men but then you don't want me laughing out loud during one of your speeches.

It's a thankless job but I've got a lot of Karma to burn off.

Some grow with responsibility, others just swell.

Stay here and finish your debate while we go off and make this a productive meeting without you.

This isn't an office. It's Hell with fluorescent lighting.

Who me? I just wander from room to room.

You are validating my inherent mistrust of colleagues.

You assign me one more action item and I'm going to show you why I play with voodoo dolls.

General put downs for any occasion

Anyone who told you to be yourself couldn't have given you worse advice.

As an outsider, what do you think of the human race?

Better at sex than anyone, now all he needs is a partner.

Did the aliens forget to remove your anal probe?

Do I look like a people person?

Do you want me to accept you as you are, or do you want me to like you?

Don't thank me for insulting you. It was my pleasure.

Don't try so hard, I couldn't like you any less.

Don't worry about biting off more than you can chew. Your mouth is probably a whole lot bigger than you think.

Don't you ever get tired of having you around?

Don't you realise that there are enough people to hate in the world already without your working so hard to give us another?

He's just visiting this planet.

Hey, I'm sorry, I'm not being rude; it's just that you don't matter.

I can please only one person per day. Today is not your day. Tomorrow isn't looking good either.

I don't know what makes you tick, but I hope it's a time bomb.

I don't know what your problem is, but I'll bet it's hard to pronounce.

I don't mind that you are talking so long as you don't mind that I'm not listening.

I know you have to be somebody, but why do you have to be you?

I know you're a self-made man. It's nice of you to take the blame!

I know you're trying to insult me but you obviously like me; I can see your tail wagging.

I like you better the more I see you less.

I like you. I have no taste, but I like you.

I see that this is the collection point for the freaks and weirdos.

I see you've set aside this special time to humiliate yourself in public.

I used to think that you were a big pain in the neck. Now I have a much lower opinion of you.

I wish we were better strangers.

I worship the ground that awaits you.

I would love to insult you, but you wouldn't understand.

I would probably find you more interesting had I studied psychology.

I'd like to have the spitting concession on his grave.

I'd like to say I'm glad you're here; I'd like to say it.

I'd like to see things from your point of view but I can't seem to get my head that far up my arse.

If I want any shit out of you I'll squeeze your head.

If I wanted to hear from an arse, I'd fart.

If there's ever a price on your head, take it.

If you act like an ass, don't get insulted if people ride you.

If you can't laugh at yourself, I'll be glad to do it for you.

If you ever need a friend, you'll have to get a dog.

I'll never forget the first time we met although I'll keep trying.

I'll swear eternal friendship for anyone who dislikes you as much as I do.

I'm not being rude. You're just insignificant.

I'm trying to imagine you with a personality.

Imagine this; I will win and you will lose. Do we need to go on?

Is there no beginning to your good taste?

Is your family happy, or do you go home at night?

It sounds like English but I can't understand a word you're saying.

I've had many cases of love that were just infatuation, but this hate I feel for you is the real thing.

Let me know if I say anything that offends you. I might want to offend you again later.

Not all men are annoying. Some are dead.

Perhaps your whole purpose in life is simply to serve as a warning to others.

Some day you will find yourself and wish you hadn't.

Someday you'll find yourself, and will you be disappointed.

Someday you'll go far, and I hope you stay there.

Thank you. We're all refreshed and challenged by your unique point of view.

The fact that no one understands you doesn't mean you're an artist.

The thing that terrifies me the most is that someone might hate me as much as I loathe you.

They say opposites attract. I hope you meet someone who is good-looking, intelligent, and cultured.

Too may freaks, not enough circuses.

Was the ground cold when you crawled out this morning?

When you were a child your mother wanted to hire someone to take care of you but the Mafia wanted too much.

Why do you have to be that way? You seemed normal until I got to know you.

Yes, I am an agent of Satan but my duties are largely ceremonial.

You are a man of the world—and you know what sad shape the world is in.

You have an inferiority complex and it's fully justified.

Your proctologist called. They found your head.

13. Sport

Sportsmen are usually more noted for their actions than their words, but being essentially a field of competition the world of sports lends itself readily to verbal attacks along with all the other volleys, kicks and punches.

· · · · · · ·

His sperm count was lower than an English cricket score.
AA Gill

The English cricket team have just three problems. They cannot bat, they cannot bowl and they cannot field.
Rodney Marsh

Cricket is a game which the English, not being a spirited people, have invented to give themselves some conception of eternity.
Lord Mancroft

Baseball has the great advantage over cricket of being sooner ended.
George Bernard Shaw

🖝 🖝 🖝

I regard golf as an expensive way of playing marbles.
GK Chesterton

No one has had a golf swing like Eamon Darcy's since Quasimodo gave up on golf to concentrate on bell-ringing.
Bill Elliot

The only time he opens his mouth is to change feet.
David Feherty on Nick Faldo

I've done for golf what Truman Capote did for sumo wrestling.
Bob Hope

When primitive man beat the ground with sticks, they called it witchcraft. When modern man does the same thing, they call it golf.
Michael Neary

Golf is a lot of walking, broken up by disappointment and bad arithmetic.
Mark Twain

***

Joe who did you say? Oh, Frazier. Yeah, I remember him. He's the one who leads with his face all the time.
Sam Bailey

Sailing, n. The fine art of getting wet and becoming ill while slowly going nowhere at great expense.
Henry Beard and Roy McKie from their **Sailor's Dictionary**

The fellows in the executive boxes at Everton [Football Club] are the lucky ones. They can draw the curtains.
Stan Boardman

Eddie Waring has done for Rugby League what [obese British MP] Cyril Smith has done for hang-gliding.
Reggie Bowden

I was a human garbage pail.
Christopher Bowman on his past drug habit

Let them find someone else to boo.
Joe Bugner on his retirement

The Extraordinary Achievement award goes to Billy Martin for having reached the age of fifty without having been murdered by someone, to the amazement of all who knew him.
Murray Chase

Football hooligans? Well, there are the 92 club chairmen for a start.
Brain Clough

John Barne's problem is that he gets injured appearing on *A Question of Sport*.
Tommy Docherty

The game is too long, the season is too long and the players are too long.
Jack Dolph on basketball

In February 1995 French soccer star Eric Cantona attacked and kicked a fan during a football match prompting one wag to make this comment:
The Eric Cantona incident was the first genuine case of the shit kicking the fan.

Skiing? Why break my leg at 40 degrees below zero when I can fall downstairs at home?
Corey Ford

Bjoring Borg … a Volvo among tennis stars.
Peter Freedman

He doesn't care about black or white. He just cares about green.
Larry Holmes on Don King

Someone with about as much charisma as a damp sparkplug.
Alan Hubbard on Nigel Mansell

McEnroe was as charming as always, which means that he was as charming as a dead mouse on a loaf of bread.
Clive James on John McEnroe

Any other problems you have besides being unemployed, a moron and a dork?
John McEnroe to a tennis fan

Football players, like prostitutes, are in the business of ruining their bodies for the pleasure of strangers.
Merle Kessler

I may have exaggerated a little bit when I said that 80 per cent of the top women tennis players are fat pigs. It's only 75 per cent.
Richard Krajicek

Managing a baseball team is like trying to make chicken salad out of chicken shit.
Joe Kulel

Martina was so far in the closet she was in danger of becoming a carpet bag.
Rita Mae-Brown on her ex-lover Martina Navratilova

He was all chin from the waist up.
Frank Moran on Billy Wells

When I was a little boy I wanted to be a baseball player and join the circus. With the Yankees I've accomplished both.
Craig Nettles

Joggers are basically neurotic, bony, smug types who could bore the paint off a DC-10. It is a scientifically proven fact that having to sit through a three-minute conversation between two joggers will cause your IQ to drop thirteen points.
Rick Reilly

Why do boys play with balls? Probably because it's the first thing they've got a hold of when they wake up.
Ted Whitten

When all else fails!

Finally, when you've tried every bit of bitchiness that you can short of physical assault here are some nasty ways of simply telling people to shut up and get lost.

● ● ● ● ● ● ●

I like long walks, especially when they are taken by people who annoy me.
Fred Allen

There's nothing wrong with you that reincarnation won't cure.
Jack E. Leonard

Every time I look at you I get a fierce desire to be lonesome.
Oscar Levant

I'd like to give you a going-away present ... but you have to do your part.

I'd like to help you out. Which way did you come in?

If I promise to miss you, will you go away?

If I throw a stick, will you leave?

I'm busy now; can I ignore you some other time?

I've only got one nerve left, and you're getting on it.

Let's go some place where we can each be alone.

Pardon me, but you've obviously mistaken me for someone who gives a damn.

Please turn off your mouth. It's still running.

And one last parting shot from Jane Austen:
You have delighted us long enough.